Managing Director Sarah Lavelle
Editorial Director Harriet Butt
Designers Alicia House, Gemma Hayden
Prop Stylist Charlie Phillips
Photographer India Hobson
Photographers Assisstant Magnus Edmondson
Head of Production Stephen Lang
Senior Production Controller Gary Hayes

Published in 2024 by Quadrille Publishing Limited

Quadrille
52–54 Southwark Street
London SE1 1UN
quadrille.com

ISBN 978 183 783 188 3

Printed in China using vegetable-based ink

THROWN

A Modern Potter's Guide to Working with Clay on the Wheel

LILLY MAETZIG

photography by India Hobson

quadrille

06 INTRODUCTION
09 HOW TO USE THIS BOOK

GETTING STARTED

12 Workspace and tools
14 Clay
18 Wedging
21 Reclaim

ESSENTIALS

24 Throwing
26 Centring
28 Throwing a Cylinder
32 Throwing a Bowl
38 Attaching bats

40 Trimming
42 Centring for Trimming
44 Trimming a Cylinder
46 Adding a Footring
48 Trimming with a Chuck

50 Handles
50 Making Pulled Handles
52 Making Slab Handles
53 Shaping and Attaching Handles

55 Decoration

58 Glazing
60 How to Make Test Tile
62 How to Mix a Glazes
65 How to Apply Glaze

67 Kilns and Firing

PROJECTS

Beginner

76 Set of mugs
79 Ridge cup
82 Saucer
86 Milk jug
91 Plate
94 Soap dish

Intermediate

98 Wide shallow bowl
103 Porridge bowl
106 Custard jug
110 Egg cups off the hump
115 Colander
118 Lemon juicer
122 Vase

Advanced

126 Candlestick
130 Teapot
138 Lampshade
144 Moon jar
150 Cake stand
154 Two-part vase

160 ABOUT THE AUTHOR
160 ACKNOWLEDGEMENTS

INTRODUCTION

As a child, I was very into making things. I would sit and make creatures out of salt dough coloured with food colouring and little cities out of lumps of black, iron-rich sand on the beach, which I adorned with shells, sticks and leaves. I would make potions in the garden from mud and various plants; I would draw endless pictures of animals, creating little worlds for them in my head.

When I was a teenager, I did as many different art subjects at school as I was allowed to do. My high school in Christchurch, New Zealand, where I'm from, had a great art department, and one year at high school I was enrolled in painting, sculpture and printmaking – fobbing off maths, science and economics to do so. I would flit around from one art classroom into another, spending my lunchtimes and free periods in there, pretending I had some deadline to meet. Really, I just loved being in spaces that were a little messy, with echoes of students before me who'd left plaster fragments in buckets and inky fingerprints on the presses.

When it was time to leave school, I didn't think about what my career might be. I just applied for a few art schools and decided to go to a local one that promised a variety of different crafts. I suppose my goal was to be an artist, like the ones that I read about in the books that lined my classrooms at high school, but the idea wasn't fully fleshed out. What kind of artist didn't really bother me – but I always wanted to be in one of those books. Being young, I worked odd jobs and took out a chunky student loan to get me through financially, still not sure where my art degree would take me.

After three years of playing with different materials and making a new best friend, I graduated as a Bachelor of Design, with a major in visual arts. Still not sure where that would take me, I decided to enrol in a pottery night class to make sure I didn't stagnate.

I was straight out of art school when I first sat down at a pottery wheel. I had this brand-new degree, actually managed to get a job at a cute wee art gallery and had big aspirations of being an artist in a book someday, although still completely blind about what that would look like.

I signed up to a night class at a local pottery club with my sister-in-law, Claire. The idea was that I was going to use the space and the kilns at the club to make sculptural pieces to keep the artist dream on track. The night class that I signed up to was pretty open: it was a ten-week, two-hours-a-week class. You could go along and use the two hours however you liked: throwing, handbuilding, glazing if you needed to. The teacher for those Tuesday nights was a wheel thrower named Terry, and on the first night, Terry did a quick demo on the wheel for anyone who fancied a go. I had no other concrete plans just yet, so I thought I'd give it a try: it looked simple enough, and I had the audacity that a shiny new art degree brings with it. I got my clay wedged up (more difficult than I'd expected), set my tools up (borrowed from Terry), put an apron on (I had made it myself), and sat down at the wheel.

Like most beginner potters, I was terrible. I was incredibly impatient and tried to blame all sorts of things for it being so difficult and my being terrible: I am left-handed, Terry did the demo too quickly, my wheel was probably wobbly, my clay had air bubbles in it.

Claire was quite good right away, so the blaming only went so far, but, luckily, I'm stubborn and a little competitive, and I stuck at it. Claire having picked it up made me see that it wasn't impossible – just hard. It wasn't until a few months later, sitting down at the wheel on a Tuesday night, that I pulled up a wall on my pot. I had pulled walls up before – but this was the first time that it didn't feel wobbly, it didn't feel like it was going to flop.

It felt smooth like butter – and I was in control of it. It blew my mind because I realized that all of the pots I'd made up to that point were lucky successes, rather than something I'd properly made happen. I chased that feeling for a while longer and would feel it more and more as I kept practising.

The pottery club I was still attending a couple of years later had a sort of open-access situation going on, and I found myself collecting tools, clay and books and then carting them all around in the boot of my car. I started an Instagram account, which, as a 21-year-old felt like my first real business move, and began documenting my progress and the pieces that I was making. When I moved to London, still in my early 20s and still armed with quite a lot of audacity, I took my 'business' with me. I rented a desk and some shelves in a shared studio and had to get good quickly because London prices were far more expensive than New Zealand ones. This was a perfect push for me to turn my hobby into a proper business, so I kept the Instagram account going, got a website, found some customers and everything grew and grew and grew.
I have now been throwing for a decade. That feeling of throwing with butter back in New Zealand led me to build a business out of pottery. I have made pieces for Michelin-star restaurants, for high-end cafés, art stores and a few exhibitions. I teach people online and in person. I have found a lovely, kind community of people who follow me on social media, I make weekly videos about the material, and I have written a book about handbuilding. I didn't mean to make pottery my career when I signed up to that night class – but that's what happened.

I hope that this book will impart some of the excitement that I feel about clay to you, and that you will feel the pure joy that comes from learning a difficult new skill.

HOW TO USE THIS BOOK

This book will teach you the fundamentals of throwing. We'll start with how you should approach your workspace and what tools and materials you'll need and then move on to how to use the wheel to throw and trim a pot and then trim it. Once you have a basic understanding, we'll dive into some projects with step-by-step instructions. I want this book to inspire you with new ideas and types of makes that you might not have tried or that perhaps you want to try a different way.

If you're brand new to clay, you can use this book from front to back, and we will go through the whole process in a linear way, but if you've spent a bit of time throwing already, you can use it like a reference book. I would love for this book to be used like a well-loved cookbook; for you to grab it with clay-covered hands in your studio or workshop so you can read up on the next step, leaving a history of your learning with each dusty fingerprint.

At every stage, I want to remind you that throwing can be difficult. It's often thrown around within the pottery community that it takes 1,000 pots for you to make a good one, so give it time. Try to keep an open and learning attitude while you're making, and create little exercises for yourself: throw 20 cups just to practice the movements, cut pieces in half to see the cross sections, say goodbye to pots that aren't great by reclaiming the clay and commit to learning over and over.

As I have been making pots for many years, and have learnt from many different people and places, I have realized that there are many different ways to do the same thing in pottery. Throughout this book, I will teach you how I do something, but bear in mind that you might like to do it differently. I highly encourage that and I'd love for you to do it my way to start with, but experiment with your own ways of doing the same thing once you've got the hang of it.

GETTING STARTED

The first part of this book is an introduction to clay – from setting up to choosing your materials. You'll learn the basics of handling the clay, and how to make it your own.

ESSENTIALS

This is the skills section which contains the fundamentals of what this book's about. Here, you'll find out how to throw and trim by learning how to make a cylinder and a bowl shape – both of which you'll need to be able to do to get your journey fully underway. Find out how to attach handles, how to decorate your pieces with texture, slips, resists and glazes and, of course, how to fire them. This is also where you'll find information about types of kilns.

PROJECTS

This is the place we all want to end up – the place where we'll actually be making stuff. Try not to run before you can walk, though. The projects are divided up into beginner projects, intermediate and advanced, and I would encourage you to be realistic about what you might make first to avoid unnecessary frustration. The very first project, a set of mugs, is still challenging if you are a total beginner, and there's plenty of scope to play around with the shapes of the mugs and the type of handle.

Remember, ultimately, if you don't like something you've made, cast it into the reclaim bucket, and start again. It's a journey.

GETTING STARTED

WORKSPACE AND TOOLS

Wherever you choose to work, there are a few basic things you need to get going.

POTTERY WHEEL

This is obviously very important! You can use either an electric wheel, or a kick wheel. I used a kick wheel for about two years when I got my first studio, and it worked very well.

To get started with your wheel, you'll need to make sure your chair is at a comfortable height, and that you have a bowl or bucket of water within easy reach, along with all the necessary tools. In all the projects, assume that I have a bowl of water with a sponge nearby. I love using a second bowl for any slops or for pots that don't make it, to make cleaning up easier.

TOOLS

There are so many tools that you could use for pottery: you can make your own, use recycled bits from around the house or, of course, you can purchase them from pottery supply stores.

To make the projects in this book, you'll need:

- Bowl of water with a sponge
- Wooden knife tool
- Needle tool
- Rib (rubber, wooden or metal – this is your preference but I like wooden)
- Teardrop loop tool
- Double-ended loop tool
- Ruler(s)
- Cutting wire
- Mirror (useful but not essential)
- Callipers (useful but not essential)

MIRROR

I like to use a mirror at the wheel to help with shaping my pots. Place a mirror in front of your wheel, so that you can see your pot and hands whilst throwing. It takes a little bit of getting used to – but will help avoid back pain from bending to look at your pot – and will give real-time feedback as you are shaping.

WATER

You'll need access to water for throwing. Make sure that the throwing water doesn't go down the sink: clay is heavier in water and can very easily clog pipes. Install a clay trap if you can. Wash hands and tools in a bucket. Let this separate in a bowl or bucket overnight, and do the same with any throwing water. Pour off the water down the drain and then pour the heavy clay into a reclaim bucket.

BATS AND WARE BOARDS

Bats are boards that go on the wheel to make it easier for you to remove your pottery from the wheel without damaging it. They are usually round, though you can get other shapes, and the size should match the size of your wheel. You throw on the bat, which is then removed, with the piece still attached, where it can dry. The idea is that if you use a bat, large or intricate pieces don't need to be removed when the clay is wet and super soft. (See page 38 for more information.)

You can also purchase tile bat systems. With this system, you get a master bat into which smaller (often square) inserts sit. You get a set of inserts with the master bat. These can be inserted and removed very easily when throwing smaller pieces. Ware boards are used to transport, dry and store your work, and they can be used for wedging and reclaiming clay, too. Plywood or MDF are popular materials for ware boards. You can use them as shelves, and move pots around your workspace easily, and can slot them into shelf systems too – with a little DIY.

STORAGE

Shelves are a must-have in a ceramics' workspace. I find that it's useful to have different categories for the shelves: drying, waiting for firing and finished. Be aware that clay is very heavy when it's wet, so your shelves should ideally be floor-standing or at least properly anchored into the walls. If you are working from home or in a shared space, try to find a spot out of the way where your pieces can dry. Dry clay is very fragile, so make sure that pieces are out of the way of being knocked or broken when awaiting the kiln.

PLASTER

An important part of pottery is recycling any pots that don't make the cut. To do this, you need a plaster bat in your studio – you place wet clay on the plaster bat, and in a few hours, it's ready to be wedged up and used again. It is very porous, and wicks water away from the clay, speeding up the drying process. Make sure it never goes into the kiln though – it'll explode!

You can buy plaster bats, but it's far cheaper to make your own. To make your own plaster bat, first purchase a bag of potter's plaster/plaster of Paris, and find a plastic tub or roasting dish to pour the plaster into. Follow the instructions on the bag to mix it up, then pour it into your tub. After a day or so, you can tip it out of the mould, let it cure for a week, and then it can be used for reclaim. Full instructions on how to reclaim can be found on page 21.

KILN

This is the most expensive item you'll need. If you're getting lessons, or working from a shared studio, you may have access to a kiln that you can use to start off with. You can also find out about shared kiln space in your area. When you feel you're ready for your own kiln, see page 67 for more on the various options.

CLAY

Clay is the main character in this book: without it, a pottery wheel is useless. It goes through a type of alchemy in the kiln, changing in the heat from something soft, plastic and pliable into one of the hardest materials around, three times stronger than steel. This is what makes clay so special. It's a simple material which is given to us by the earth, yet it holds such potential within it.

TYPES OF CLAY

Today, the most common type of clay that you will find in most potter's studios is purchased from a pottery supplier. However, clay is naturally occurring, and can be dug up from the ground. This is known as wild clay. If you are a beginner, I suggest purchasing clay from a supplier before going down the road of experimenting with wild clays – they are exciting but can be very unpredictable.

Before choosing your clay, you need to decide what you want from your pieces. There are three basic types of clay that you can use on the wheel: earthenware, stoneware and porcelain.

EARTHENWARE

Firing temperature: In the range of 950–1100°C (1745–2012°F or cones 010–03). This makes it a low-firing clay. The very top range of earthenware is 1200°C (2195°F or cone 5), although at this temperature, the clay will start to bloat and melt.

Finish: Terracotta is a type of earthenware known for its rich red colour, but earthenware can be purchased in a wide range of colours, from white to red. It can be either very smooth or with some grog, a pre-fired pottery that has been ground down to the texture of sand to strengthen the clay, mixed in.

Decoration: Because of earthenware's low firing temperatures, you can decorate your pieces with bright colours using slips, underglazes and stains (see page 55).

Cost: Firing your kiln at a lower temperature means that it requires less energy (and therefore less money!) as the kiln has an easier time getting to temperature.

Durability: Earthenware is much less durable than stoneware or porcelain. It also tends to melt before it reaches proper vitrification (no longer porous), so this leads to earthenware being less ideal for functional ware. Using a glaze can help this but water can get trapped within the ceramic and grow bacteria and mould – so keep an eye out for this. Earthenware's porosity gives it better thermal shock properties than stoneware, and therefore earthenware is better to make oven-safe items with. Always use this with caution.

STONEWARE

Stoneware is split into two categories: mid-firing and high-firing.

Firing temperature: Mid-firing clay temperatures are in the range 1160–1240°C (2120–2264°F or cones 2–7); high-firing clay temperatures are around 1263–1326°C (2305–2418°F or cones 8–12).

Range of colours: Stoneware can be purchased in a range of colours, from white to grey or buff. It's possible to purchase coloured stoneware clays also. These clays have been coloured with pigment and are not naturally occurring.

Decoration: Because stoneware is fired hot, any surface decoration tends to be more muted and earthy than on earthenware. In saying that, there are many slips, underglazes and oxides which can handle firing to very high temperatures, although the range is more limited (see page 55). Using a mid- rather than high-firing clay will allow you to achieve brighter colours.

Cost: Firing to the very top ranges of stoneware requires a lot of energy and the price to power a kiln is much higher than for earthenware.

Durability: Mid-firing stoneware, although stronger than earthenware, can be on the soft side and doesn't always vitrify in the kiln. I very often see potters using stoneware clay but firing it too low. When this happens, moisture can build up between the layer of glaze and ceramic and grow bacteria and mould. High-fired stoneware generally does vitrify around 1280–1300°C (2336–2372°F), leaving you with durable, dishwasher- and food-safe pieces.

PORCELAIN

Firing temperature: Porcelain is the highest-firing clay body, with its upper limit being around 1350°C (2462°F or cone 13). This temperature is walking the line of porcelain's melting point. This means that there is high risk of warping and cracking. But, with great risk comes great reward: the unique, beautiful glassy properties that porcelain offers, requires that it is taken this high.

Range of colours: Porcelain is known for its pure white colour, although colourants can be added.

Decoration: Like stoneware, porcelain's colour palette is limited because of the high firing temperatures required. However, because porcelain is such a white clay, any colours applied to the surface tend to be vibrant.

Cost: Both the clay and the firing are expensive.

Durability: Porcelain is very strong and, when fired to high temperatures, is very durable. Generally, potters like to throw thinly with porcelain to produce its distinctive translucency. Doing this can create pieces which may break easily if dropped. Pieces are also more liable to warp and crack in the kiln than earthenware and stoneware, so you should be aware of this, too.

Tip

If you're making functional ware, make sure the clay that you're using is being fired hot enough. I often see potters using a high-firing clay, but not firing it to maturity, meaning that it's not reached its top temperature. The result is that the fired ceramic is softer than it should be, leading to easy breakages, chips and cracks. It will also hold onto water and bacteria because it is not vitrified. If you want to fire lower, make sure the clay is designed for that.

DIFFERENT STAGES OF CLAY

Clay goes through different stages on the way to becoming ceramic, and a little understanding here will help you when you come to make the projects.

GREENWARE

This is the term for all the different stages of clay before it has been in the kiln. All greenware can be recycled (reclaimed), so offcuts or pots you don't want to fire can be added to your reclaim bucket to be turned into something else. More information about reclaiming can be found on page 21.

Wet clay: This is clay with a high water content. Clay should be soft, mouldable and squishy when you are working with it on the wheel. It can be made into almost anything at this stage, although there is a limit to what you can do with wet clay, as you may have experienced when a pot flops on the wheel.

Leather hard: This is a wet clay that has dried out for a while. You can tell when a piece is leather hard: it's the same colour as wet clay, but it's no longer squishy or tacky. You can make a mark on it easily by, for example, scratching it with a fingernail, but it is rigid. This is an important stage for working on the wheel, as it's when you trim your pieces, add texture or attach things like handles or spouts. You can keep your clay at the leather-hard stage for a few weeks if you wrap it properly.

Bone dry: Once all the water has evaporated from the clay, it will become hard and very brittle. Be very careful with your pieces at this stage: if you pick up a piece by a rim or handle, you may snap the clay. It's possible – but very difficult – to reattach broken pieces once the clay is bone dry. Your pieces are ready to go into the kiln once they are bone dry.

ADDITIVES

You can add certain materials to your clay – or purchase your clay with these additives pre-mixed in – to change the finished look and properties of your work. Popular additives are grog, sand and paper.

Grog and sand: These have similar properties and can help improve strength and add texture. You can add up to approximately 5% for this purpose. Grog is ground-up ceramic that has been pre-fired. Sand is the regular beach kind, although you may want to purchase sand from your pottery supplier for consistency as sand collected from a beach can be contaminated with other substances. If you do use sand from the beach, be sure to test thoroughly for colour, contaminants and texture. Both grog and sand can add things like speckles or beautiful textures to your pieces. Sand can also be added to glaze.

Paper pulp: This can be mixed into clay to create paper clay. This is done to give greenware strength, as well as making it more repairable, making it popular for sculptural work with loads of joins or attachments. Once fired, the paper will burn off, leaving the pieces very light. You can buy paper clay, or make your own with toilet paper, newspaper or cardboard. Paper clay grows mould very quickly and makes for very smoky firings, so beware of this when working with it.

SHRINKAGE

All clay shrinks when it goes through its drying and firing processes. This is because wet clay contains approximately 20% water, and when that water evaporates, the clay particles fuse closer together. Most clays shrink somewhere around 5–15%, and it's really helpful to know exactly how much a clay body will change. To find out more, you should perform a shrink test.

Note

It is easiest to use centimetres for this test as you can very quickly turn the amount of shrinkage into a percentage – as you will quickly realize, it's much more complex if using fractions of an inch.

DOING A SHRINK TEST

1. Roll out a small slab of clay. Measure 10cm (4in) and cut out a little rectangle.
2. Turn your clay into a ruler by marking each 1cm (⅜in) up to 10cm (4in).
3. Fire the clay to the temperature you usually fire to.
4. Using a regular ruler, compare the size of your new ceramic ruler.
5. If you find that your ceramic ruler now measures 9cm (3⅝in) on your regular ruler, you can see that it has shrunk 1cm (⅜in) i.e. 10%.

If you're making pieces that you want or need to be a specific size, such as a candlestick or a saucer for your favourite cup, or if a client has asked for the same size as a piece they already have, you now know that you need to add 10% onto your pieces to allow for shrinkage.

BISQUEWARE

A bisque firing is the first firing that bone-dry pieces go through to become ceramic. A bisque is around 1000°C (1832°F or cone 06). During this firing, all excess water is removed from the clay and it goes through a chemical change to become ceramic.

When you unload the kiln, you will notice that your pieces feel different. They are likely to be a little lighter, they may have shrunk a little (see opposite), and may have changed colour. Your pieces will also be very porous at the bisque stage – on a microscopic level, the bisqueware is literally like a sponge, with open capillaries ready to drink up any liquid.

This is when you can glaze your pieces. There is more on glazing on page 58 but, in short, a glaze is a type of glass suspended in water. The bisqueware soaks up all the water and leaves behind a glassy layer on the surface of the ceramics. Once a piece has been glazed, it can go back into the kiln for its final firing, where the glaze will melt and fuse to the surface of the ceramic, and the ceramic itself will ideally reach maturity, with all the tiny particles fusing tightly together. Through this firing, the piece will shrink a little bit more too. (You can find out more about the firing process on page 67.)

WEDGING

Wedging is a very important process in which the clay is mixed and air bubbles are removed. The process aligns the clay particles in a uniform pattern, stacking them up like bricks and creating a lovely body to throw with. Removing air from the clay is very important – trapped air in the clay can push a piece off centre, create little tears, and cause small cracks and blisters on the surface of fired pieces.

Clay should always be wedged in preparation for throwing, whether you are using clay straight from the bag or whether it's reclaimed clay.

The most common wedging techniques are ram's head and spiral. Always work on a surface that the clay won't stick to, such as untreated wood or canvas.

RAM'S HEAD WEDGING

This is the most common technique for beginner potters to learn. It's very effective for small (200–1000g/½–2¼lb) amounts of clay, and it gets its name from the shape it makes.

1. Pat the clay into a general ball shape and then use both hands to pull it up on its edge with your fingers.
2. Position your hands facing down on the clay, fingers facing away from you. Push the clay down and away from yourself with the balls of your hands, with even pressure going through both palms. Press your hands down as well as in towards each other at the same time to ensure the clay isn't just rolling into a flat shape. If this happens, concentrate on pressing in rather than down.
3. Repeat 20–50 times, until you can cut the piece of clay in half with a wire without seeing any air bubbles.

SPIRAL

Spiral wedging is my preferred wedging method. It's great for wedging smaller pieces (200g/7oz) and even up to quite large (2–5kg/4½–11lb) if you have the upper body strength.

1. With both hands on the clay, pull it up on its edge with your fingers.
2. Press the clay down and away from you with the ball of your dominant hand. Your non-dominant hand helps with applying pressure, as well as making sure it doesn't spread too wide. The hard work is done with your dominant hand.
3. Bring the clay up onto its edge, turn it 10–15°, and repeat step 3. If you are right-handed, you will turn the clay anticlockwise, if you are left-handed, you will turn it clockwise.
4. Repeat 20–50 times, until you can cut the piece of clay in half with a wire without seeing any air bubbles.

Tips

- Use both your body weight and your arm strength to wedge.
- Do not fold the clay, as this will create potential for bubbles to be added. Rather, you're trying to press the clay into itself to remove air.
- Once you are into the movement of wedging, you will feel that it is a fluid, rocking motion.

▼ SPIRAL – STEP 1

▼ SPIRAL – STEP 2

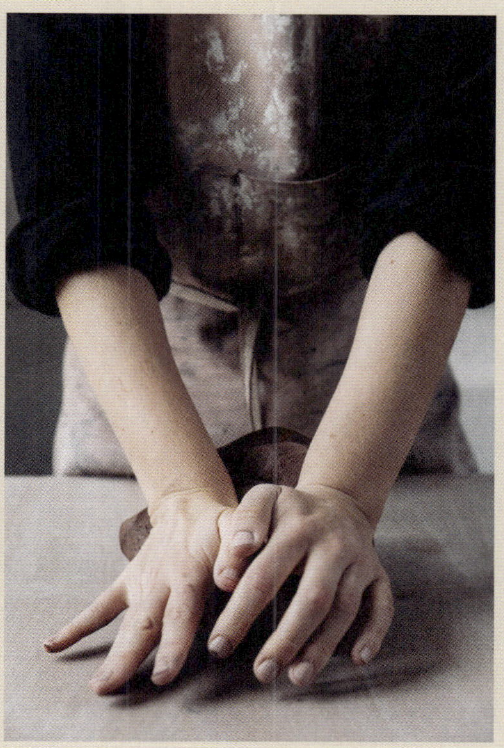

▲ SPIRAL – STEP 3

▲ SPIRAL – STEP 4

▼ STEP 1

▼ STEP 2

▲ STEP 4

▲ STEP 5

RECLAIM

'Have nothing in your house that you do not know to be useful or believe to be beautiful.'

William Morris

Learning to throw is a very long process, and it is something that many beginners get very frustrated with. I also see beginners get very attached to pots that survive the throwing stage, and fire pieces that realistically they won't find either useful or beautiful once they are through the kiln. Not being able to look at your pieces with a critical eye, and wanting to keep everything you have made in the very early stages can stunt genuine learning and growth. You can take a photo of the pieces made, or only keep really special ones, but there is something very liberating in thanking the clay for what it's taught you and then giving it to the reclaim bucket to become something else.

In a world where there are already so many things, we, as makers, have a responsibility to be mindful of what else we add. It's a very special aspect of clay that if a piece doesn't go through the kiln, it can be reclaimed infinitely, so clay that has been used to learn the basics of centring, for example, can be the same clay that teaches you the basics of attaching handles. All offcuts and scraps can be reclaimed too, making clay a very environmentally friendly material. I am very careful and critical about which pieces make the firing stage – if I see a crack in a handle or think that a form isn't quite right, it goes from the drying shelves straight into the reclaim bucket. This saves time, resources and mental energy trying to fix it (or trying to like it!) later.

HOW TO RECLAIM CLAY

Reclaiming in fairly small batches makes the task less overwhelming.

1. While you're throwing, keep a bowl or bucket nearby to fill with slops and pots that don't make it. These can be placed on a plaster bat to dry a little, before being wedged up to use again the same day; you can keep them wrapped up to wedge another time; or you can add them to the reclaim bucket. Keep trimmings and other scraps, like extra handles or pots that aren't going to be fired, and add them to your reclaim.
2. When the bucket is filled up with dry or drying clay, you can submerge the clay in water. Leave it for at least a week.
3. Mix the clay with your hands (if you can handle the feeling!) or with a drill with a paint mixer attached.
4. Transfer it from your bucket to some plaster bats, anywhere up to 5cm (2in) deep. The plaster pulls the water from the clay.
5. Press your fingers into the reclaim to create some small wells in the clay – this helps with airflow and can speed up the drying.
6. Once the clay has dried enough that you can peel it up from the plaster, flip it over and let the other side dry a little.
7. Roll the clay and wedge it up. See wedging on page 18. If you don't have time to wedge now, you can wrap your clay tightly in plastic for another time.

ESSENTIALS

THROWING

Throwing can be quite difficult to wrap your head around when you first begin. As the wheel and the clay move, it's your job to guide it into the pot that you want it to be by slowly, patiently and confidently coaxing the clay into place.

The basic mechanisms of throwing are:

- Centring
- Opening
- Pulling up the walls
- Shaping the walls
- Refining and finishing
- Removing from the wheel

Centring is explained in more detail on page 26 and the instructions for making a cylinder (page 28) and a bowl (page 32), two fundamental shapes, will take you through the other stages. Although each step is important, getting the centring right is the most vital.

THE BASICS

There are a few things to consider before you actually start throwing.

DIRECTION OF THE WHEEL

The direction in which the wheel spins is usually determined by your dominant hand. In this book, I will be referring to the western right-handed way of throwing, where the wheel is spinning anticlockwise. I will be referencing hand positions as if the wheel head is a clock, so if you are left-handed and want to throw with the wheel spinning in the clockwise direction, mentally adjust the clock-face recommendations accordingly.

Having said this, I am left-handed, and I learnt how to throw with the wheel moving anticlockwise because I didn't know that there was any difference. You will always be using both hands for throwing, and I don't think there is any time where hand dominance really comes into play when doing this. When you're learning a new skill, all the movements will feel unnatural and foreign to you, so it may be less complicated to learn as the steps state, than to have to convert to left-handed instructions. Experiment with what feels best for you.

POSITIONING

To give your hands greater stability, you should anchor your forearms on the splash pan or your legs when throwing, and then keep them locked in this position.

USING THE WHEEL

Ensure the wheel is moving fast enough to make one full rotation before you move your hands. Then think about the speed at which you move your hands.

You can control the speed of the wheel, usually with a pedal. When centring, you should go fast, opening and pulling up the walls should be at a medium speed, and for refining and finishing go slow. You should always have your foot on the pedal ready to slow the speed for something more intricate or to remedy an issue.

It's very tempting to follow the clay around as it moves on the wheel, especially if you make a mistake and want to fix it. As you spend more and more time throwing, you'll learn that there is only a very small area where you need to work to make a pot, which is somewhere between 3 and 6 o'clock on the wheel head.

Make sure that the wheel is always moving when you are touching the clay. I see beginner potters often stop the wheel to try and straighten a wall or fix a rim. Once in a blue moon this will work, but more often than not it will exacerbate the issue. It may also develop into a bad habit and bad technique.

CENTRING

Centring is the very first process that happens when you are throwing a pot on the wheel, and arguably, it's the most important. It's the process of pushing the clay into the centre of the wheel to ensure that you are creating a symmetrical piece. Centring is difficult to learn, so be very patient with yourself – you may spend five or ten minutes trying to get the clay centred when you're starting out. But after some practice, you'll get your technique worked out, and you'll be able to centre in a matter of seconds.

Materials and tools

Clay, approx. 300–400g (10½–14oz)
Sponge and water

Tips

- Use the weight of your upper body to assist you. Hinge at the hips over the top of your wheel. You don't need to be super strong to centre clay, but your arm and hand muscles benefit from the extra help.
- Use loads of water to keep the clay lubricated. Without enough water, your hands will create friction with the clay and it will be pulled off centre.
- When removing your hands from the clay, do so slowly, and keep the wheel moving, so that the clay doesn't stick to you and pull off centre.
- If your hands are being pushed around by the clay, you're not applying enough force. Remember you are controlling the clay – the clay isn't controlling you.

1. Take your wedged ball of clay and pat it into a ball shape. Using the concentric rings on the wheel head to guide you, place your clay onto the dry wheel head, as close to the centre as possible. Firmly slap the clay down with the heel of your palm so it adheres to the wheel head.
2. Turn the wheel on and hold the index finger of your right hand against the base of the clay at around 5 o'clock to seal it to the wheel head.
3. Wet your hands and the clay. With the wheel spinning reasonably fast anticlockwise, anchor your elbows on your splash pan or legs, and firmly cup the clay with your hands. Squeeze your fingers towards the heel of your palms, and your palms towards your fingers. Make sure that both hands are always touching each other to ensure they are working as a team. Continue to wet your hands and the clay as needed throughout this process.
4. With the heel of your left hand, apply pressure firmly towards the top right of your wheel; your right hand should be firmly pressing down, towards the wheel head. Squeeze the clay in and move your hands up to form a cone shape with the clay.
5. Create a right angle with your hands and, with even pressure through both hands, repeat the movements, but this time guide the clay back down to the wheel head.
6. Repeat this whole process two or three times, until you have an even puck of clay and you can no longer see or feel the clay wobbling – neither on the top or side of the ball of clay.
7. You'll be able to tell when you've got the clay centred, as it will feel still – you won't be able to feel it moving under your hands, or you won't be able to see it dancing around as the wheel is moving.

▼ STEP 4

▼ STEP 5

▲ STEP 6

▲ STEP 7

THROWING A CYLINDER

A cylinder is one of the best foundation pieces that you can make as a potter. It's more technically difficult than a bowl, but practising this shape over and over again will lead to a great understanding of the basic skills that are needed for throwing, and bowls should come easier after this. You'll learn how to centre, open, pull up a wall, shape and remove your piece effectively by throwing cylinders over and over again.

Materials and tools

Clay, approx. 300–400g (10½–14oz) for each cylinder
Wooden rib
Wooden knife tool
Cutting wire
Needle tool if you need to remove the rim
Sponge and water

Note

To achieve height with your cylinders, you must work against the centrifugal force on the clay caused by the wheel spinning. The clay wants to flare outwards. Concentrate on creating cone shapes when you're pulling up your walls – aim for an imaginary point high above your pots where you might close this cone shape. Your pot can be shaped when you have achieved the height you are aiming for, but usually by the third pull the walls are straight or slightly tapered out anyway.

It's worth preparing loads – say 20 – balls of clay to throw cylinders, and committing to not keeping any of the finished pieces, in order to practice.

1. Centre the clay following the instructions on page 26.

OPENING

2. Use your left hand as a support, cupping the clay. Place your right thumb on top of your left hand and then, using this thumb as a hinge point, slowly press the index and middle fingers of your right hand into the centre of the clay until you reach approximately 1cm (⅜in) away from the wheel head.
3. Widen this opening by crooking your fingers and dragging them approximately 2cm (¾in) towards you, working from the very centre of the clay down towards 6 o'clock. Ensure that you are dragging your fingers parallel to the wheel head to create a flat base.
4. Compress the base by moving the pads of your index and middle fingers across from the middle to 3 o'clock a few times. You can also do this with a damp sponge. Compressing the base will reduce the risk of S cracks, as well as making sure you have a neat interior to your pot.
5. Collar the walls a little by cupping the whole shape, and gently squeezing the clay into a volcano shape.

PULLING UP THE WALLS

Your left hand will now move from a supporting role on the outside of your pot to becoming a key player on the inside of your pot. You will be working around 5 o'clock – do not move higher than 3 o'clock, as tempting as it may be. Keep your elbows anchored to the splash pan, or tucked into your body to stay stable.

6. Ensure the clay and your fingers are wet, and get the wheel moving at a medium speed.
7. With your left hand, create what I like to think of as a 'dog' shape by resting the pads of your middle and ring fingers on the pad of your thumb. With this shape, hold your hand

vertically, and place your fingers on the inside of the pot at 5 o'clock, where the base meets the wall. Place your thumb, still in this 'dog' shape, opposite your fingers on the outside of the pot, resting where the clay meets the wheel head. Your thumb will naturally land a little lower than where your fingers have landed. With the pads of your index and middle fingers on your right hand, support your left thumb. Rest the thumb of your right hand on your left hand to anchor them together.

8. When you're in place, gently squeeze the clay as you slowly move your hands up towards the rim. The wall will grow as your fingers move up the clay. Note that the walls are most sturdy at the base, but as you approach the rim, the clay becomes more waterlogged, softer and more delicate. It's easy to tear the rim, so as you get to about two-thirds up the wall, ease the pressure off. Keep your fingers moving up the wall until there is no more clay to pull up.
9. Apply slightly more pressure with your outside fingers when pulling your walls up to create a cone shape. If your pot is beginning to flare outwards, collar it in by cupping the pot at the base, and gently moving your hands up the wall. (For more information about collaring, see page 37.)
10. Compress the rim by placing the thumb and forefinger of one hand on either side of it (not squeezing) and pressing down onto the rim with the index finger of your other hand.
11. Repeat steps 7–9 two or three more times, until you have achieved the height that you want.

SHAPING

12. Repeat step 11 two or three times until you have achieved a shape that you're after. If the rim is wonky, you can simply remove it with the needle tool (see below).
13. You can use a rib to shape your pots. I use the straight edge of the rib to guide my straight-sided pots. Hold the rib with your right hand, and think of the tool as an extension of your fingers, and gently press the clay into the side of the rib, slowly moving both your fingers on the inside, and the rib on the outside of the pot. Rest your left thumb on your right to keep your hands moving as one. If your rim is wonky at this stage, jump down to step 12 on page 35 for a tip on removing your rim.

FINISHING

14. Hold the wooden knife tool in both hands against the base of the pot to remove any excess clay where it meets the wheel head. This also creates a nice notch for the cutting wire to glide through without damaging the base of the pot.
15. Wring out your sponge and gently move it from the middle across to 3 o'clock on the interior base of the pot to remove any excess water or slip. You may need to repeat this a couple of times to remove all water.
16. Repeat step 10 once more to compress the rim – this helps ensure a strong rim.
17. Stop the wheel from spinning. Wring out your sponge on the wheel head at 12 o'clock.
18. Hold the cutting wire taut and, with your thumbs, press down into the wheel head. Pull the wire through the water and under the pot, ensuring it drags the water through. The pot will begin to slide.
19. Remove the wire and slide the pot from the base off the wheel. Gently place it onto a ware board. Ensure you handle it as little as possible, and where you do need to handle it, make sure it's from the strongest point (i.e. the base, rather than the rim).
20. You did it! Repeat this whole process many times over to practice.

Remember that this is a practice cylinder, so you can now cut it in half to examine the thickness of the base and the walls. You're aiming for a consistent thickness from the base all the way up the walls to the rim.

▼ STEP 1

▼ STEP 2

▲ STEP 7

▲ STEP 8

▼ STEP 3

▲ STEP 13

Tips

- If it's easier, you can open with your thumbs instead of forefingers. To do this, cup the clay with both hands and press both thumbs evenly into the clay.
- If you're having trouble gauging how thick the base of your cylinder is, you can place a needle tool all the way into the base until it reaches the wheelhead. Mark where the needle and clay meet with your finger. As you remove the tool from the base, your finger will show you the depth of your base. If you have less than 5mm (¼in) you could wire right through the base as you remove your pot from the wheel. If it's thicker than around 2cm (¾in), you'll need to trim a lot of excess clay off the bottom of your pot later. Aim for a consistent 1cm (⅜in) for cylinders.
- When you're pulling up the walls of your cylinder, you may find that they are flaring out. Ensure that you are focusing on making a cone or volcano shape by applying more pressure with your outside fingers than your inside fingers.
- Some potters use the knuckle of their right hand or a sponge instead of their thumbs and pads of their fingers when pulling up the walls. I never had luck with those techniques, but if these work for you, continue doing this.
- Train your fingers to feel where the clay is thicker or thinner and adjust the pressure that you apply as you work. This will help you achieve even walls on your pots.
- If you leave water inside your pot, the walls and base will dry unevenly, and the base will crack.
- Practice, practice, practice! Learning to throw is a skill, like learning to speak a new language or to play an instrument. It's difficult but you will get there with commitment.

THROWING A BOWL

After you've made a few cylinders, you'll find that bowls come much more easily. They are simpler forms to make, but in my opinion slightly harder to master. With a bowl, you don't have to fight so hard against the forces trying to bring the clay outwards, because that's where you want the clay to go, but you now need to contend with gravity and work with the limits of the clay to keep the bowl from flopping. Bowls and cylinders share very similar starting points.

Materials and tools

Clay, approx. 350g (12½oz) for each bowl
Wooden rib
Wooden knife tool
Cutting wire
Needle tool if you need to remove the rim
Sponge and water

1. Centre the clay following the instructions on page 26.

OPENING

2. Use your left hand as a support, cupping the clay, and place your right thumb on top of your left hand. Using this thumb as a hinge point, slowly press the index and middle fingers of your right hand into the centre of the clay, until you reach approximately 2.5cm (1in) away from the wheel head.

3. With your hands in the same position, create a tiny bowl shape on the inside of your clay, by gently pressing the clay from the middle of the opening, up towards 4 o'clock until you reach the rim. This can be done a few times, much like compressing the base for the cylinder.

4. Collar the clay in a little bit by cupping it with both hands and bringing your hands from the base to the rim. This will establish a cone or volcano shape.

PULLING UP THE WALLS

As when throwing a cylinder, work at around 5 o'clock and don't move higher than 3 o'clock (see the instructions for the cylinder on page 28). It's important with a bowl to achieve the height that you want before you begin to widen it out into a bowl shape. As before, ensure the clay and your fingers are wet and have the wheel moving at a medium speed.

5. With your left hand, create the 'dog' shape from page 29 by resting the pads of your middle and ring fingers on the pad of your thumb. With this shape, hold your hand vertically, and place your fingers on the inside of the pot at 5 o'clock. To get into position, rest the pads of the fingers of your left hand in the centre of the opened pot, with your left thumb and the finger pads of your right hand where the clay meets the wheel head.

▼ STEP 1

▼ STEP 2

▲ STEP 5

▲ STEP 7.1

▼ STEP 7.2

▼ STEP 9

▲ STEP 11.1

▲ STEP 11.2

6. Your thumb will naturally land a little lower than where your fingers have landed. Rest the thumb of your right hand on your left hand to anchor them together.

7. Squeeze the clay as you slowly scoop your inside fingers from the centre to where your thumb is resting. When you've reached your thumb (this is what will become the shoulder) both hands can start moving up the side of the wall, towards the rim. The wall will grow as your fingers move up the clay. As with cylinders, it's easy to tear the rim, so as you get to about two-thirds up the wall, ease the pressure off. Keep your fingers moving up the wall until there is no more clay to pull up.

8. Collar the walls in to re-establish the cone shape (see step 9 for the cylinder on page 29).

9. Compress the rim by placing the thumb and forefingers of one hand on either side of it (not squeezing) and pressing down onto the rim with the index finger of your other hand.

10. Repeat step 7 and 9 two or three more times until you have enough height and it's started to become bowl-like.

SHAPING

The shoulder needs enough clay beneath it for the pot to stay upright – if it's unsupported, it will succumb to gravity and flop. You can trim off the excess clay later.

11. With the same motion as pulling up, you can begin to shape your pot. This time, you won't be squeezing the clay but instead gently pressing outwards as you move up the side of the pot. Both hands should be working in unison. You can use a rib tool or a sponge to help you shape at this stage.

12. Repeat step 11 two or three times until you have achieved a shape that you're after. If the rim is wonky, you can simply remove it with the needle tool (see page 36).

FINISHING

13. Follow the finishing instructions for the cylinder (page 29) to remove any excess clay where it meets the wheel head, sponge off excess water or slip and compress the rim once more. Cut your bowl from the wheel and place it onto a ware board.

See the tips for cylinders on page 28, which also apply to making bowls.

▼ STEP 3

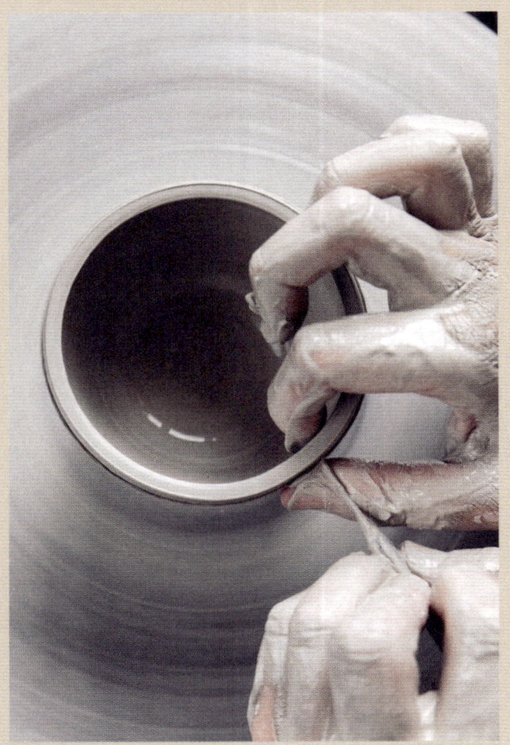

▲ STEP 4

THROWING TIPS

REMOVING THE RIM

If the clay is not centred, or you are pulling your walls up too quickly, you may find that the rim goes a little wonky. It's possible to remedy this by removing the rim altogether while the pot is still on the wheel. You'll need a needle tool for this. The technique can be scary the first few times you do it. Make sure you have a firm grip of the needle, quite close to the tip. If not, it can flick itself out of your grip and cut the pot – or you!

1. Hold the needle tool firmly with your dominant hand.
2. Wet the index finger and thumb of your non-dominant hand, and place these either side of the rim, about 3mm ($^{1}/_{8}$in) lower than the lowest spot at about 6 o'clock.
3. With the wheel spinning slowly, rest the needle tool against your thumb on the outside of the rim and very slowly poke the needle tool into the rim.
4. When you reach your finger on the other side, you can gently remove the rim.
5. Compress the rim to re-establish the round shape and to clean it up.

COLLARING

While you are throwing, you and the pot are playing with (and fighting) centrifugal force, which is pulling the clay outwards – if you've ever spun the wheel too fast, you may have been witness to a dramatic ripping apart of the clay, and a big mess to clean up. Potters can use wheel speed to play with this force, but collaring is a way to bring back a pot that has started getting a little too wide, and it's used when making things like bottles, vases and lemon juicers as well.

It is basically the hugging of the clay and guiding it towards an imaginary point at the top of a cone. For larger pieces of clay, you can use your whole hands, while for smaller pieces, or more detailed areas like a bottle neck, you can collar with the pads of your thumbs, index and middle fingers. To do this, slowly squeeze the clay towards the centre, starting at the base and moving up the walls of the clay. The clay may go into a funny triangle shape when you are doing this, but once you remove your fingers, you'll see that the clay has magically changed its direction.

Collaring won't save every pot that's started getting too wide, but it's a great tool to use to stop things from getting out of control.

USING A HEAT GUN

A heat gun is a tool that many potters use to speed up the drying process and make their pieces leather hard quickly. You can also use one to make wet clay a little firmer, so if you're making large pieces the clay is less likely to flop.

Although I do have a heat gun, I very rarely use it. I find it can create uneven drying and cause shrinkage issues. It can get incredibly hot very quickly – around 600°C (1112°F). Be careful where you direct the heat and of the surfaces that you place it down on, and take care not to touch the hot end of it.

ATTACHING BATS

Bats are boards, usually round and made of wood, that attach to the wheel head, and they are especially useful when you're making very fine, large or wide pieces. Once you have finished throwing a piece, you remove the whole bat from the wheel, instead of attempting to move the pot and potentially damaging it.

Some wheel heads have special attachments or little screws for bats to slot into, but if your wheel head doesn't have any, you can throw a thin layer of clay directly onto the wheel, called a pad. Here's how.

Materials and tools

Clay, approx. 150g (5¼oz)
Wooden rib
Bat
Sponge and water

1. Wedge the clay up and centre it directly onto the wheel head.
2. Centre this ball of clay down flat and wide, until it is about 0.5–1cm (¼–⅜in) thick. Tidy the pad and remove the slip by holding the flat side of a wooden rib against the pad.
3. Create a ring of clay in the middle by holding your finger in one spot and letting the wheel spin.
4. Repeat step 3, approximately 2cm (¾in) below the previous ring, until you have created rings across the whole pad. It will look a bit like a clay target.
5. Remove much of the water and slip from the pad with your sponge then place your bat on top of the pad, centred. You can use the edges of the wheel head to help you place it.
6. To stick the bat down, create a fist, and with your thumb facing the ceiling then thump the bat into place while the wheel is slowly spinning. If your bat slides off, you can add a little extra water to the pad and repeat this step.
7. Throw your cylinder, bowl or pot directly onto the bat in the same way as when working directly onto the wheel head. However, when you are about to wire through the base, ensure you do not drag water through as you might on the wheel head. Excess water under the pot can make it difficult to remove when it's leather hard.
8. Let your pot dry to the leather-hard stage and it will release itself from the bat when it is ready. Having said that, sometimes very wide pieces like plates can be hard to remove – they may need to be wired through when it's leather hard to release.

▼ STEP 2.1

▼ STEP 2.2

▲ STEP 3

▲ STEP 6

TRIMMING

Once your cylinder, bowl or pot has hardened to leather hard, it's time to trim it. Trimming, also known as turning, is the process of removing excess clay from your piece and refining it. To do this, your pot is centred once again on the wheel, but this time upside down. Once you get the hang of trimming, you can really change the look of your thrown pot, for example, by trimming in a footring.

In this section, we will cover the fundamentals of trimming, and use our thrown cylinders or bowls from before to get us started. Cylinders can be tidied up, and the excess clay removed, while bowls look great with a footring trimmed into the base. Of course, both cylinders and bowls can have whatever finish you decide once you've practiced.

Trimming is my favourite part of the whole throwing process – you may not enjoy it to begin with, but eventually it will become very satisfying to see how much your piece can change at this stage.

Note

If your piece is not centred from throwing, it will be difficult to centre it for trimming. Do your best to get the base centred, and you can ignore the rim.

TOOLS

You can use loop tools and chisel tools for trimming, or some people use ribs. I generally use a double-ended loop tool, with one square end and one round end, plus a bigger teardrop-shaped one. I encourage you to have a play with different types to see what you like best.

I liken my trimming tools to a highlighter or permanent marker with a chiselled end in that you can change the type of marks you make with it depending on how you hold it. For example, if you hold the corner of a square loop tool against the clay, a deep but narrow mark will be made, and if you hold the flat part to the clay, a wider but shallow amount of clay will be removed.
Hold your trimming tool at approximately 45° against the clay. Hold it with both hands to keep it steady, as it's very easy to lose your grip and gouge the clay.

I will be using a large teardrop and a double-ended loop tool for my instructions. You can use whatever you have, and adapt to these instructions, although these are basic tools that tend to come in most starter toolkits.

MEASURING THE BASE

When you are trimming your pieces, you should aim to have the base and the walls the same thickness. It's important that you know the thickness of your base so that you trim enough excess off, without going through the bottom.

To measure your base, place your piece on a flat surface and lay a flat tool across the rim. Hold a ruler or another tool vertically inside the pot, resting the tip on the base, in the very middle.

Hold the vertical tool at the point where it meets and move it to the outside of the pot, resting it against the flat tool again.

The space between the wheel head and the tip of the vertical tool shows how thick your base is.

As you get more experienced, you'll be able to get to know the approximate thickness of your bases without checking every time, but as a beginner, it's worth making checking a habit.

CENTRING FOR TRIMMING

There are a few ways to secure your pot to the wheel for trimming. Using lugs is very popular, both for beginners and experienced potters, and I would suggest using them while you get used to the trimming process (see Technique 1 below).

I am a fan of sticking my pieces to the wheel by suction. It's a slightly riskier technique, as pots can easily unstick and fly off the wheel (disaster!) but I find that the reward outweighs the risk once you have the technique down (see Technique 2).

There are also tools which you may like to use, such as the Griffin Grip, which hold your piece in place, but I dislike these tools for most uses.

Materials and tools

Clay, approx. 50g (1¾oz) if using lugs
Leather-hard piece for trimming
Sponge and water

TECHNIQUE 1: USING LUGS

1. Take the clay and break it into three small bits. Roll these into little caterpillars and place them aside.
2. Lightly wet your wheel head with the sponge. Turn your leather-hard cylinder (or whatever piece you are working with) upside down.
3. Use the concentric rings on the wheel to help locate where the middle of the wheel is and place the cylinder as centrally as you can.
4. Check if the cylinder is centred by slowly spinning the wheel and holding your finger in one place. If the cylinder taps your finger, and then moves away from it, it is not centred. Move it a tiny bit at a time away from the spot where it tapped your finger.
5. Repeat this step until the cylinder is centred: once it does not tap your finger but stays pretty solidly in one spot and touches your finger most of the way around, it's centred. It may take a few minutes of practice. Turn off the wheel.
6. Take the three caterpillars of clay (lugs) and press them into the wheel head where it meets the rim of your cylinder. Space the lugs evenly around the cylinder then press the clay down into the wheel head rather than into the rim, as this can cause warping or cracking. You can use more lugs on larger items.

TECHNIQUE 2: USING SUCTION

1. Lightly wet your wheel head with the sponge.
2. Take your leather-hard cylinder (or whatever piece you are working with) and turn it upside down.
3. Use the concentric rings on the wheel to help locate where the middle of the wheel is and place the cylinder where it looks centred.
4. Slowly spin the wheel and hold your cylinder at the same time. Swirl your cylinder around a little as the wheel spins to create some slip.
5. Slow the wheel spin right down and check if the cylinder is centred by holding your finger still in one place. If the cylinder taps your finger, and then moves away from it, it is not centred. Slide it a tiny bit at a time away from the spot where it tapped your finger – don't lift it up as this will remove the suction seal that you've just created.
6. Repeat this step until the cylinder is centred: once it does not tap your finger but stays pretty solidly in one spot and touches your finger most of the way around, it's centred. Gently tap the base of the cylinder as the wheel is spinning to make sure it's well adhered.

Tips

- When using Technique 2, you might find that centring is difficult as the cylinder can become really quite stuck during step 4. With wide hands, firmly but carefully press the cylinder away to get it to slide, being mindful that it may unstick and fling off! It takes practice and finesse to get this down.
- To unstick your cylinder from the wheel after trimming, use this wide-hands trick again but with the wheel moving as slowly as possible. You just need to push it off centre and it will unstick, although sometimes the rim can get damaged doing this. Tidy up any wobbles with a damp sponge.
- I would avoid doing this technique with pieces that aren't well centred to begin with, those that have uneven thickness (thin at the rim especially) or ones that are overly dry.

▼ TECHNIQUE 1

▲ TECHNIQUE 2

TRIMMING A CYLINDER

For the cylinder, we will only remove excess clay and tidy it up. It doesn't matter which loop tool you use for this exercise – give both a go to see what they can and can't do, and see if you have a preference. There are three areas to concentrate on: the base, the walls, and the area where the base meets the walls, which I will refer to as the shoulder

Materials and tools

Leather-hard cylinder
Loop tool of choice
Sponge and water

Tips before you begin

- Be mindful of the speed of the wheel whilst you are trimming. If the wheel is moving too slowly, and your hands are moving too quickly, you will create spirals on your pot. Your hands must move at an appropriate speed to the wheel – giving it enough time to complete a full rotation before you move your hands.
- As a general rule, hold your tool parallel to each area when trimming. The shoulder will be a 45° angle to create a chamfer (see step 7).

1. Take your leather-hard cylinder and centre it for trimming (see page 42). Spin the wheel at a slow speed and select a loop tool to try.
2. Begin by removing excess clay from the shoulder by holding the loop tool against it until you have removed any clay that is flaring outwards.
3. Next, flatten the base. Hold the tool against the base of the pot at a 45° angle. Start in the very middle and slowly move your tool down towards 5 o'clock. Apply more pressure in the middle than the outside to give a very slight convex shape to the base.
4. Now even up the walls by holding the loop tool parallel to the walls and slowly moving from the base down towards the rim. Apply enough pressure to remove the excess clay, but be mindful that the pot may slip, so be ready to catch it with your left hand. Repeat this until you are happy with the shape of the pot.
5. You don't have to trim all the way down to the rim, but if you want to you can trim until you reach the lugs. You can finish the area you can't reach later by hand.
6. To finish the pot, repeat step 3, but this time hold your tool at approximately a 45° angle to create a chamfer. This chamfer helps the finished piece to look refined – it elevates it just a tiny bit off the surface when it is finished.
7. Remove all the clay trimmings from the wheel head and dust your hands off. Wring your sponge out until it is slightly damp and, at about 5 o'clock, slowly move it from the middle of your pot, all the way down until you reach the lugs.
8. Remove the lugs by peeling the clay away from the wheel head, and gently remove your pot. Tidy up any messy areas and the rim with your sponge, then stamp or write your name in the base.
9. Leave your piece to dry or wrap it up if you want to add a handle later. Repeat this over and over again: the first few times may feel very frustrating, but eventually you'll be able to trim your cylinders very quickly.

▼ STEP 2

▼ STEP 3

▲ STEP 6

▲ STEP 8

ADDING A FOOTRING

This is my favourite task. It's not just tidying up your piece, but allowing it to become something quite different from what it was when it was thrown. I like to add a footring to a bowl, but it can be put on a cylinder too, if you choose. It can be as wide as the base, or you can shape the exterior of the bowl and carve a footring into it.

The process is a little more difficult than the previous exercise. I use two different loop tools for this task, the double-ended tool and the larger teardrop – but you can use whatever you have and adapt these instructions to your tools if need be. Make sure you have enough depth in the base of your bowl to carve in a footring. Check the depth using instructions on page 40.

Materials and tools

Leather-hard bowl
Teardrop loop tool and double-ended loop tool
Sponge and water

1. Take your leather-hard bowl, and centre it for trimming following the steps on page 42.
2. Spin the wheel at a slow speed. Using the teardrop loop tool, begin by removing excess clay from the shoulder by holding the loop tool against it until you have removed any messy clay that is flaring outwards.
3. Next, flatten the base. Hold the tool against the base of the pot at a 45° angle. Start in the very middle, and slowly move your tool down towards 5 o'clock.
4. Switch to the double-ended loop tool and use the square side. Holding the tool steadily with both hands, rest one corner of the square loop still against the base of the bowl, approximately 2cm (¾in) from the very middle. This will draw a circle on the clay.
5. Do this again, approx. 1.5cm (⅝in) away from the first circle, towards the edge of the base. This has created two circles on the clay. You will next remove clay from both sides of the double circles, leaving a ring in the middle.
6. Very firmly hold the round end of your double-sided loop tool on the outside of the second circle to create a bit of a trench in the bowl, around 1cm (⅜in) deep.
7. Remove all the excess clay on the outside of this trench.
8. In a straight line down towards 5 o'clock, drag either side of the double-sided loop tool from the very middle out to the first circle. Make sure you're holding your loop tool with both hands.

Repeat this process a few times until you have removed 0.5–1cm (¼–⅜in) of clay. You will be left with a footring!

9. Use any of your tools to tidy up the rest of the bowl, especially the shoulder area. Try to match the internal shape to the external shape.
10. You don't have to trim all the way down to the rim, but if you want, you can trim until you reach the lugs. You can finish the area you can't reach later by hand. Remove all the clay trimmings from the wheel head and dust your hands off.
11. Wring your sponge out so it's slightly damp, then drag it slowly from the middle all the way over the side of the pot to smooth it off. Remove the lugs by peeling the clay away from the wheel head, and gently remove your pot.
12. Tidy any messy areas and the rim up with your sponge, then stamp or write your name in the base. Leave your piece to dry on a flat surface.

▼ STEP 5

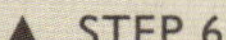
▲ STEP 6

▲ STEP 8

TRIMMING WITH A CHUCK

A chuck is something that you can attach to your wheel head to trim pieces that have a narrow rim that won't stick to the wheel head without support, such as a bottle. Chucks are usually thrown.

To make a chuck, throw a thick cylinder that is wide enough at the neck to fit your piece into, and narrow enough to hold it in place. It must also be tall enough for the shoulder of the piece that you are trimming to rest on, and it should have a thick rim.

Leave your chuck to get to the leather-hard stage before using it. Attach it to the wheel head the same way as you would anything else for trimming, centring it and using lugs to stick it down. Your piece must then be centred on it – lightly dampen the rim of the chuck to ensure the pot sticks.

Chucks can be kept for a long time. I wrap my chuck well in plastic, and have had the same one for a couple of years – I've become very attached to it! Some potters bisque-fire their chucks, but I prefer the stickiness of a leather hard one.

You can also be creative with what makes a chuck. I have used buckets and plant pots for very large pieces: I drape a cloth or some tissue paper between the chuck and the pot to stop it marking the walls of the pot. Generally, larger pieces weigh the clay down enough so that no lugs of clay are needed to stick it to the chuck itself.

See a chuck in action in the lemon juicer project on page 118, candlesticks on page 126, and moon jars on page 144.

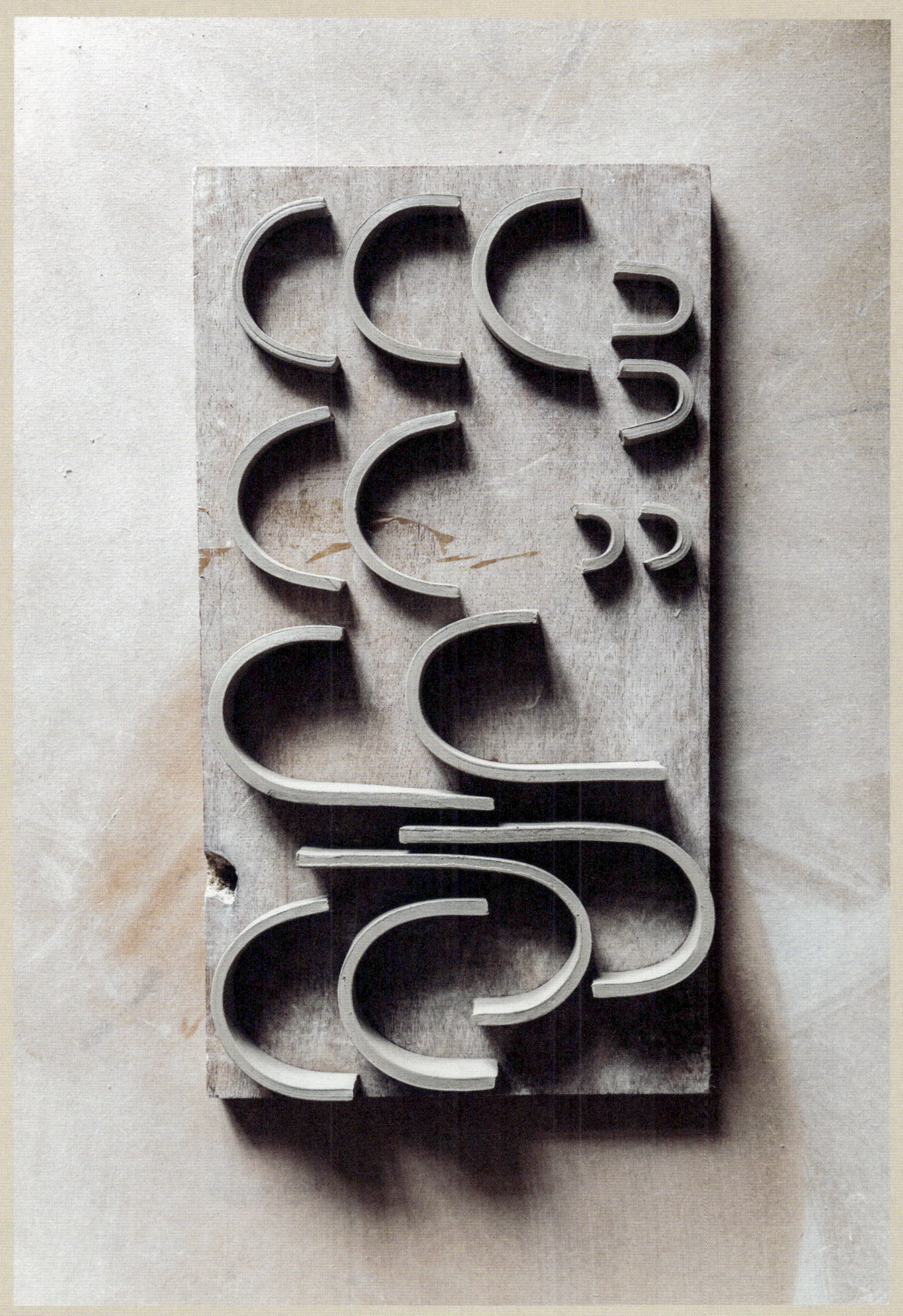

HANDLES

Attachments can completely change the appearance and function of a piece: adding a handle to a cylinder suddenly makes it a cup, or adding a spout to a vase changes it into a jug. They are also a fun way to add character to a piece. Many larger pots have handles just to elevate them.

Pulled handles are traditional, whereas squarer slab handles have a modern simplicity that may suit your work. Our first exercise in attachments will be adding a handle to a cylinder to make a cup or mug.

MAKING PULLED HANDLES

The process is a little like milking a cow – which, admittedly, I haven't ever done – but that may help you imagine the hand movement. The instructions are for making a batch of handles at the same time.

Materials and tools

Soft wedged clay, approx. 500g (1lb)
Slip
Plaster or wooden board
Wooden knife tool
Serrated rib and needle tool for attaching the handles
Sponge and water

Tips

- Leave these lengths of pulled clay to dry a little on the board for approximately 15–30 minutes to harden up a tiny bit.
- If a large, bulbous piece of clay forms at the end, gently pinch this off and set it aside, then continue with your pulling.

1. Roll your clay into a cone shape. Hold the thicker end of the cone with your non-dominant hand then squeeze the bottom of the cone into a shape that you grip entirely with your dominant hand.
2. Wet your hand and the bottom of the cone with your dominant hand.
3. With your dominant hand, grip the end of the cone and firmly pull the clay down. Applying consistent pressure all the way from the top to the bottom, you will notice the clay stretching down. Slide your hand all the way to the bottom of the cone on each pull. To shape the pulled clay, you can squeeze your thumb closer to your fingers, and flip the whole clay cone 180° with your non-dominant hand when needed.
4. Once you have a long piece of clay that feels like it would be a good width of handle, gently lay the end on your board, and pinch off lengths approximately 10cm (4in) long.

▼ STEP 2

▼ STEP 3.1

▲ STEP 3.2

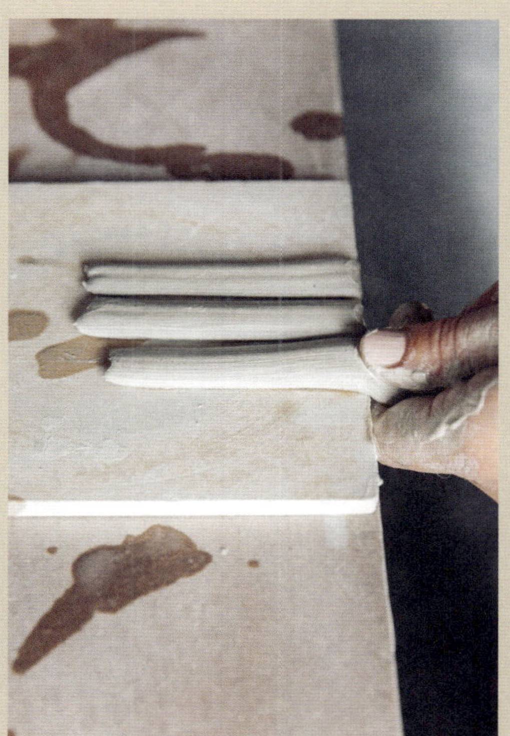

▲ STEP 4

▼ STEP 1

▲ STEP 2

MAKING SLAB HANDLES

Slab-made handles are less traditional for thrown pieces. For years, I pulled all my handles, but one day I realized that my work is very square by nature, with lots of straight lines. Pulled handles have a softer quality to them, and the square nature of slab handles suits my work more.

Materials and tools

Soft wedged clay, approx. 500g (1lb)
Slip
Plaster or wooden board
Rolling pin
Wooden knife tool
Ruler
Serrated rib and needle tool for attaching the handles
Sponge and water

1. Roll out slab of clay to around 5mm (¼in) thickness with a rolling pin.
2. Using a ruler, cut a long strip of clay, approximately 1cm (⅜in) wide and 10cm (4in) long.
3. Gently bend the clay into a handle shape and hold it up to the side of your cup, then decide on the profile that you are looking for. Trim the handle down to size – it may end up much smaller than 10cm (4in) long.
4. If you are making, say, a set of cups, use the rest of the slab to cut out handles to the same size as your first handle and gently bend them to shape.

SHAPING AND ATTACHING HANDLES

Shaping a handle can be done either before or after it is attached to the cup. Have a play around with what you like the look of. If you like the traditional half-heart shape, you should opt for shaping once you have attached it.

SCORING AND SLIPPING

Scoring and slipping is the method that is used to attach one piece of clay to another, whether you're adding a handle or a spout or joining clay in a handbuild. You want both pieces of clay to unite and become one.

First you score both sides of the join, which helps the clay grab and hold. Then you add the slip. Slip is clay with a higher water content – more of a liquid than a solid – and it acts as the glue when attaching scored pieces of clay. The clay must be firmly pressed into place so that when it dries, the join doesn't fail and the handle or spout doesn't fall off.

SHAPING ON THE CUP

1. Decide where you'd like the top of your handle to sit on your cup and score this area on your cup with a serrated rib.
2. Apply a blob of slip to the scored area. Take a recently pulled handle and tap the top of it lightly to create a wide surface area. Gently score this with either a serrated rib or a needle tool.
3. Press this end of the handle onto the cup where you have scored. Support the inside of the cup with your other hand to avoid misshaping it.
4. Blend the join with your finger but be mindful of gravity pulling the tail of your handle in funny directions and try to avoid this.
5. Once the top of the handle is blended, gently bend the tail of the handle down to the spot where you want it to sit.

▼ STEP 3

▲ STEP 4

▼ STEP 4

▲ STEP 6

SHAPING OFF THE CUP

1. Shape your handle when it is wet enough to do so, either by eye or using something like the rounded shape of a rolling pin to do this. Allow the clay to dry to leather hard.
2. Decide on the final placement of your handle. Hold it up to the side of the cup. With your needle tool, mark where the top and bottom of your handle will sit on the cup.
3. Trim your handle so that the top and tail will sit flush on the cup and score both sides.
4. Score the cup on the two spots that you marked in step 2.
5. Apply a generous blob of slip to the top and tail of the handle, then firmly press the handle onto the side of the cup, supporting the inside of the cup with your other hand to prevent cracking or warping.
6. Using your fingers or the back of the wooden knife tool, gently blend the clay from the handle into the side of the cup. Tidy up the joins with a very lightly dampened sponge.
7. Dry very slowly: drape a piece of plastic over the top of your newly handled cup to ensure even drying of the handle and cup, which will help the join stay strong.
8. Be sure to not pick the cup up by the handle until it has been fired – it will snap off.

DECORATION

COLOUR

You can decorate your pots by applying colour in a variety of ways. Colour can be found naturally in the clay or added to it, or it can be applied as a coating afterwards by brushing it on, pouring it, dipping or spraying. Whatever colourants you are working with, make sure they are rated to the temperature you are firing your pieces to: earthenware is generally fine for most colourants, but stoneware is fired hotter and colours may disappear altogether in the kiln.

OXIDES AND STAINS

Oxides and stains are the raw pigments that coloured clays and glazes get their colour from, and they can be mixed with water or painting medium and applied to the clay. You can mix just 1–10%, into water or medium for great results.

Oxides can be used on clay at any stage, on bisqueware, and even on top of unfired glazed ware if you are very careful with application, but beware of how you handle your pots after applying oxides or stains as it's very easy to smudge them when they are dry.

Note

Oxides are less stable than stains, and some can be toxic. There are ethical issues with some too, such as cobalt. Always research if you aren't sure which oxides can be harmful and always wear a good-quality mask when using powders.

SLIP

Slip is liquid clay mixed with pigment and is a type of paint for your pieces. It is always used on wet or leather-hard clay, as it shrinks at the same rate as your clay: if you apply it to dry clay or bisqueware, it will shrink unevenly and may flake off.

Slips can be layered up, as long as the prior layer is dry to the touch. It can then be carved into, or stencils can be applied to mask out areas to make interesting patterns or to draw pictures on the surface.

UNDERGLAZES AND ENGLOBES

Underglazes and englobes are similar to slip, but they have a small amount of fritted material added to them so they melt a tiny bit when they are in the kiln. This means that they shrink a lot less than slip alone and are much less likely to flake off. It also means that you can apply underglaze to pieces that have already been bisque fired. It's possible to layer more colour onto already fired slips or straight onto the ceramic. Underglaze is more expensive than slip but also more versatile.

CERAMIC PENCILS

Ceramic pencils are made from oxides and will survive the heat of the kiln, unlike regular pencils, which will always fire out at high temperatures. The finished look is like that of a regular pencil. Use them on bisqueware. Usually a translucent glaze would be applied over top.

Pastels and crayons are also available, and are used in the same way as ceramic pencils.

GLAZE

The last way to add colour to pieces is by glazing them. Glaze is applied to bisqueware and is fired to very high temperatures. Glazing has its own section (see page 58).

THROWING LINES

The easiest way to get texture is to throw it in!

1. Throw a pot.
2. Slow the wheel speed down and hold your fingers as if you are about to pull up a wall or shape the pot.
3. Being mindful of the slow wheel speed, you can quickly pull your fingers up the side of the pot to draw an exaggerated wavy texture into the pot.

TEXTURE

Texture is a great way to add interest to your pieces. For thrown pots, the most common way to add texture is to carve a pattern into your clay, but you can also use stamps, texture rollers or even found objects, including leaves and flowers, bark, stones and items from the home which you can press into leather-hard clay. You can add texture on the wheel, too.

CARVING

There are many ways to carve. Throw a thick pot, and, after trimming it, use a trimming tool to make a pattern on the surface. Faceting and fluting are traditional and effective ways of carving a pot, and these create bold shapes by literally cutting new facets into your piece to change its shape. If you apply a layer of coloured slip first, you can carve patterns or drawings into the pot. This is called sgraffito.

STAMPS

These can be pressed into the surface of your clay to create regular relief patterns. Stamps can be handmade from bisque-fired clay or wood, or they can be purchased. Rubber stamps work, but not as well as harder stamps. Press these into the leather-hard clay after throwing and trimming.

▼ THROWING LINES

▲ WAX RESIST

FLANGE AND WAVY RIM

Like faceting, adding a flange or creating a wavy rim changes the form of your piece. The rim on this pot was thrown in, just like the pot before.

1. Throw a pot and identify the size of rim that you would like.
2. Create a flange. Hold the index finger of your right hand against the exterior of the pot, and very gently fold down the top of the rim over your finger. Don't pinch the clay while doing this, as it may lead to the clay being too weak and tearing.
3. This has created a flange. You can stop here if you like the look of this and then tidy it up with a rib.
4. To create the wavy rim, brace the underside of the flange with your right thumb and forefinger and bring the index finger of your left hand through the space between, gently pressing down.
5. Repeat this action around the entire flange.
6. When the clay has hardened to leather hard, you can sponge down the waves to soften any harsh fingermarks.

See both the wavy rim and the straight flange turned into lampshades on page 143.

WAX RESIST

Because slips and glazes are water-based, you can paint wax onto your pieces and it will resist the liquid, leaving blank areas.

This is most often used to protect parts of your pieces or the kiln shelves from unwanted glaze drips. However it is a great decoration tool, too. You can paint the wax into patterns or pictures, and the colour of the glaze will contrast with the colour of the fired ceramic.

This technique works on both green- and bisqueware, and the wax will burn away in the kiln.

GLAZING

Glaze is the finishing touch on most fired pots. It's the shiny coating that you see on commercial tableware that's basically a very thin layer of glass. Having said that, it doesn't always have to be shiny – it can be anything between shiny and matte, and it can have interesting textures, colours and finishes.

Glaze is often used for decoration, but the function of a glaze is to help strengthen the piece and help keep tableware hygienic. It can also waterproof porous pieces.

Usually, glaze is applied to pieces at the bisque stage (having been fired somewhere around 1000°C/1832°F), when the pots are porous. The piece will then go into the kiln again and will be fired hotter than this to allow the glaze to melt and the ceramic to harden further. See the section on clays on page 14 for more information about this.

THE SCIENCE

Glaze is made up of four main elements: silica, flux, a refractory element to stiffen up the mix and colourant(s).

Silica: This is the glass former in the glaze, and all glazes will contain it. It's also known as quartz or flint in recipes.

Flux: Silica has a very high melting point, so flux is added to the glaze to bring down that melting point. Two types of fluxes are added to glaze. The first is usually in the form of feldspars or nepheline syenite. The second type is one of the following: calcium carbonate (whiting), magnesium silicate (talc), strontium, barium or zinc.

Refractory component: A refractory material is added to the mix to harden everything up and to help stick the glaze to the surface of the pot. The ingredient that is needed here is alumina, and it's usually added in the form of a powdered kaolin (china clay) or ball clay. This is different from the body clay you make your pots with.

Colourants: If you make a glaze from the right combination of the above ingredients, you'll get a clear glaze. To add colour, various pigments, minerals, stains or oxides must be added in very small quantities. They don't tend to change the chemical make-up of the glaze.

When you are starting out, you can experiment with store-bought glazes to understand what you like and dislike, before slowly starting the journey into creating your own glazes. You'll also learn how to use glaze before spending a small fortune on glaze materials.

After experimenting with commercial glazes, you may decide you'd like to make your own by following a recipe. There are loads of recipe resources available, in books and online.

TEMPERATURE

When buying a glaze or looking for a good glaze recipe, make sure the clay you are using is rated to the same firing temperature as your glaze. Doing this will ensure that you have optimal glaze fit, meaning that your pots and glaze will shrink at the same rate and won't leave you with any glaze defects like crazing (cracking in your glaze) or crawling (missing spots of glaze on your pieces).

TESTING

To begin your glazing journey, I would suggest making some test tiles or sacrificing some pots to trial your glazes on. There's nothing worse than risking a whole batch of pieces to a new glaze and it turning out terribly – it's heartbreaking as well as wasteful.

HOW TO READ A GLAZE RECIPE

Here is an example of a glaze recipe:

40	potash feldspar
30	silica
20	calcium carbonate
10	kaolin
100	
+ 12	zirconium silicate

Glaze recipes can seem confusing the first time you encounter them. The numbers along the side denote a percentage, which should always add up to 100%. You'll notice there is an extra 12% added – this is a colourant, which does not count towards the chemical make-up of the glaze, and so it is written as an addition.

The recipes are written like this so that you can create any amount of glaze that you'd like. If you wanted to make 1 kilogram (2¼lb) of glaze, you would multiply this recipe by 10, creating 1000g (35oz) of finished product.

When you multiply the sample recipe above by 10, it will be as follows:

400g (14oz)	potash feldspar
300g (10½oz)	silica
200g (7oz)	calcium carbonate
100g (3½oz)	kaolin
1000g (35oz)	
+120g (4¼oz)	zirconium silicate

In my experience, it is very tidy working with grams for glaze recipes as it is simple to create large quantities when working with multiples of 10. However, any recipe can be converted to pounds and ounces if desired.

The glaze recipe above is a simple, balanced and stable glaze at cone 10 (1280°C/2336°F). Most glaze recipes have many more ingredients which can look confusing and overwhelming, but just remember that they should be written as a percentage and they will feel more approachable.

HOW TO MAKE TEST TILES

There are several ways of making test tiles. This is the method I use.

Materials and tools
Clay, 1–2kg (2¼–4½lb)
Bat
Wooden knife to create texture (optional)
Sponge and water

1. Centre the clay on the wheel, flat and wide, following the instructions on page 26.
2. Create some donut shapes: divide the clay into two or three channels by opening the clay up in the middle all the way to the wheel head. Space the channels between 1–3cm (⅜–1¼in) apart.
3. Pull the clay in the middle channel up until it's approximately 5cm (2in) high. Leave enough clay on either side of the wall, so it is in either an L or T shape.
4. Repeat this with the other donuts of clay.
5. Tidy up these walls. An optional extra is to hold a wooden knife against the outside of the walls to create a line – this will enable you to see how the glaze looks on both flat and textured clay.
6. Wire through the base and allow the clay to dry to leather hard.
7. Once your donuts are leather hard, slice them into approximately 2.5cm (1in) wide tiles.
8. Tidy the tiles with a sponge and let them dry.
9. Bisque-fire the tiles and store them until you're ready to test your glazes on them.

When testing, I like to dip the tile in my glaze for about 2–3 seconds, and then dip a single corner into the glaze again. This enables me to see if I like the look of a thin or thick application.

You can also test different glazes overlapping each other. Go wild with your tests and see what you like the look of.

Always label the base of your test glazes with a ceramic pencil and note down the test in an app or a notebook. Glazes can change so much in the kiln that it can be very difficult to remember what you've tested!

▼ STEP 3

▼ STEP 7

▲ STEP 8

HOW TO MIX A GLAZE

Safety first

When working with glaze powders, always use a good-quality, well-fitting dust mask rated for use with silica (at least FFP3, N95 or above) or a filtered respirator. Prolonged exposure to silica dust can cause an irreversible lung disease known as silicosis. Ideally work outside, or use studio extraction or at the very least, open a window, to reduce the risk of inhalation and the amount of dust in the studio.

Materials and tools

Two buckets: bucket 1 with a sealable lid (so you can save the glaze for later use) and both buckets large enough to hold both the glaze powder and added water

Scales – I use digital kitchen scales

Glaze powder: use a commercial glaze or mix up your own (see page 59)

Water, at least the same weight as the glaze (weigh it to ensure the correct amount)

Sieve, at least 80 mesh

Mixer – I like to use a kitchen scrubbing brush, but a rubber spatula or a paintbrush works too

Stick blender or drill mixer (optional but useful, especially when working with large quantities of glaze)

SET-UP

1. Put your mask on and prepare your glaze area.
2. Place bucket 1 (the bucket with a lid) on the scales, then tare (zero) the scales. Add the glaze powder to the bucket. If you are making your glaze from scratch, you need to measure each ingredient out and add it to the bucket. If you are using a commercial powder glaze, add that to the bucket. Note the weight of the glaze.
3. Pour around ¾ of the water all over the glaze. Note how much water you are adding every time you pour some in.
4. Let the water soak into the powder for a minute or so before mixing the glaze.
5. If the glaze is very thick, like pancake batter, you may need to add a bit more water at this stage. Once you have mixed through all the lumps, place the sieve on top of bucket 2. Use the stick blender here if you want to.
6. Pass the glaze through the sieve and into the second bucket. You can do this in a few batches if there is too much glaze to fit into the sieve. Use your brush or spatula to push the glaze through the sieve.
7. Pour a little extra water into bucket 1 to get any extra glaze off the sides and base of the bucket, and mix that up. Pour that through the sieve and into bucket 2.

8. Give the glaze in bucket 2 a quick mix, then dip your finger into the glaze. Generally, you are looking for the consistency of double cream. If it's very thick, add a little more water.
9. Place the sieve on top of bucket 1. Pour the glaze through the sieve and back into bucket 1, adding any last water to bucket 2 to get rid of any glaze stuck on the sides. Dip your finger into the glaze again and determine if it is the desired consistency.
10. You can now start glazing or put the lid on the glaze to seal it up until you are ready to use it.
11. Note down how much water you used to achieve the thickness of double cream. Some glazes need 1:1 water, but some need less and others need more. It is important to note how much water you added so that you can replicate the glaze when you next mix it up, or amend the amount of water if you didn't get the results you wanted with this mix.

▼ STEP 6.1

▲ STEP 6.2

▼ POURING AND DIPPING STEP 3

▼ POURING AND DIPPING STEP 4.1

▲ POURING AND DIPPING STEP 4.2

HOW TO APPLY GLAZE

Glaze can be applied in a few different ways: by brushing, pouring and dipping or spraying. It is usually applied to bisqueware – a piece of clay that has gone through the kiln once, to about 1000°C (1832°F).

If you've opened a bucket of glaze before, I'm sure you will have spotted a layer of water on top, with a thick layer of glaze particles at the bottom. The glaze particles are heavier than water, which is why they eventually sink. Before you glaze, ensure that you've stirred up your bucket well for a few minutes.

You may notice big lumps in your glaze, especially if it's a bucket you've not used for a while. If you notice lumps even after mixing make sure you sieve the glaze into another bucket before using. Ensure you keep stirring the glaze frequently while you're using it, too.

If you haven't used a particular glaze before, it's good practice to test it on some tiles first so you can see how it looks when it's thin and thick, as well as when you dip it twice. If using brush-on glaze you may wish to test up to three layers.

If you have had your bisqueware sitting around for a while (a few weeks or months), then you may find it's very dusty. You can wash bisqueware to make sure you achieve good glaze adhesion. Give it a rinse in a bucket of water or under the tap, and let it dry for at least 24 hours before glazing.

BRUSH-ON GLAZES

Brush-on glazes can be purchased from pottery-supply companies. They have the same ingredients as other glazes but tend to be less watery and generally have an added gum medium to make them easier to apply. You will also need glaze brushes, which have very soft bristles and can be loaded up with a lot of glaze at once.
As always, test your glaze before committing to your prize pots, then apply it as follows:

1. Stir your glaze well and ensure your bisque-fired pot is clean and free of dust.
2. Brush the glaze on the inside of your piece before the outside and apply a couple of layers, if needed.
3. Remove glaze from any unwanted areas with a damp sponge and ensure the base of the pot is well sponged clean or your pot could stick to the kiln shelf.
4. When touching unfired glazed ware, make sure you have dry hands – wet hands will pull the glaze off the surface.

POURING AND DIPPING

Pouring and dipping are sisters and best friends, an iconic glazing duo. It's the most common way of glazing in studio pottery, as it's a very efficient and simple way of applying glaze to pots. It's my go-to method.

You can get specialist glazing tongs from ceramic supply companies, and dip the whole pot using these. I have never liked that – and prefer to just use my hands! You can try both, though, and use whichever method works best for you.

1. Make sure your bisque-fired pot is free from any dust on both the inside and outside.
2. Mix the glaze well with your mixing brush then dip your jug into the bucket and scoop up some glaze.
3. Pour the glaze into the pot and leave it for two to three seconds. Some glazes need more or less time than this – determine this with your test tiles. If you are glazing a cup, you can fill the cup up. If you are glazing something larger, like a wide bowl, slowly and carefully swirl the bowl to cover the entire interior of your pot.
4. Pour the glaze back into the bucket then leave your pot upside down for a few seconds to allow any excess glaze to drip off.

5. If the pot is very thin, you may notice that the outside appears wet. Leave the pot overnight to allow the excess water to evaporate from the ceramic.

6. Holding the bottom of the pot tightly, dip the pot rim down into the bucket of glaze. The rim will form an air pocket in the glaze bucket, meaning that the glaze won't be applied a second time in the interior. Dip the pot or cup however deep you would like the glaze to go to – for example, a half-dip, two-thirds of the way up or fully submerged. Ensure you hold the pot level, as holding it on its side may cause the trapped air to escape, leaving a messy application as the air disturbs the liquid. Keep the pot submerged for the same length of time as when you poured glaze into its interior – two to three seconds.

7. Remove the pot or cup from the glaze and give it a firm shake to flick any drips off the rim. If the glaze looks better when it is thick, you may want to dip it a second time.

8. Turn the pot up the right way again and carefully place it down. If the glaze is a slow-drying type, you may need to slide the pot carefully to the side of your workbench to avoid touching the freshly glazed surface.

9. Top up any fingermarks by dipping your finger in the glaze and dabbing it onto the pot. Don't smear it on – this will remove glaze.

10. Once the pot or cup is dry to the touch, remove any areas of unwanted glaze with a damp sponge. Make sure you remove all the glaze from the base or the pot could stick to the kiln shelf.

11. When the piece is completely dry, you can tidy up drip marks or pinholes by lightly brushing a dry finger over the area. This is called fettling. If you are doing heavy fettling, wear a mask and work in a ventilated area.

SPRAYING

Spraying glaze isn't my forte – I don't have a spray booth in my studio, so I don't use this method. However, if you have access to a spray booth, it's a great way to glaze larger pieces or to get interesting glaze effects.

Glaze spray guns are slightly different to standard spray guns. If you have access to one, I recommend asking for an induction to help you understand how to use it properly.

You must also work in a well-ventilated area – ideally a spray booth with extraction – and wear a properly fitting respirator.

1. Mix your glaze well for a few minutes, and pass it through a sieve to make sure there are no lumps.

2. Set up your spray booth. Place a banding wheel in the booth and your bisqueware on top of this.

3. Set up your spray gun following the instructions for your gun. This includes filling up the glaze tank. Do a few test sprays to make sure it's working properly.

4. Spin the banding wheel and spray the glaze onto your work, ensuring that you move the spray gun in a consistent movement to get an even layer of glaze onto your piece.

You can also use something called a siphon glaze blower. This is like a spray gun but you power it by blowing into it. It's suitable for smaller amounts of glaze. Set it up the same as you would for a spray gun.

SANDING BISQUEWARE

I never sand my bisqueware. But if you're unhappy with the surface of your piece, you can do so, making sure you wet sand it as the dust created from sanding a pot is very hazardous to breathe in. After wet sanding, your piece will need to be thoroughly washed and left to dry for at least 24 hours before glazing.

Many potters do sand their work, but I would suggest working on the surface of your pieces before they are fired, at the leather-hard stage, rather than having to sand them later.

KILNS AND FIRING

The process of 'cooking' the clay in a kiln is called firing, and this needs to happen at high temperatures. Kilns are specifically made to reach incredibly hot temperatures – far hotter than your oven at home, or even a commercial oven. Clay must go through a chemical change in the kiln at over 500°C (932°F) called quartz inversion. This is the point of no return with clay, and it becomes ceramic around this stage. Before then, you can recycle the clay.

After a decade of making ceramics, I still feel like a delighted little kid on my birthday every time I unload a glaze kiln. It's one of the great rewards of ceramics.

TYPES OF KILN

There are a handful of different ways to fire your pieces, some very old, some much more modern. We will start with the modern methods that you are more likely to use.

ELECTRIC KILNS

This is probably the most common type of modern kiln, especially for craft potters. Electric kilns are lined with kiln bricks, which are special bricks that can withstand the heat of the kiln, and coils of elements. They're either a top-loader or a front-loader, and the lid or door will also be lined with kiln bricks. They're usually cased in stainless steel.

Newer kilns will have a thermocouple on the inside, which is the internal temperature probe. This is a very sensitive piece of equipment, and care must be taken not to knock it while loading or firing. It feeds the controller and will let you know what temperature it is during the firing.

Older kilns will have a sitter. A cone is placed in the sitter, which will bend when it reaches a certain temperature. Once the cone bends, a switch is flipped within the sitter and this will end the firing. Many kilns will have peepholes so you can check how the firing is going. These should be plugged at around 600°C (1112°F).

Glaze firings in an electric kiln are also known as oxidation firings, as there is oxygen present in the kiln.

GAS KILNS

Gas kilns are still very widely used within the pottery world. They use propane or natural gas and, like an electric kiln, are lined with refractory kiln bricks. There are no elements in a gas kiln, but instead it has burners and uses a draft system to control the heat.

A real benefit of a gas kiln is the ability to control the atmosphere that your work is exposed to, which affects the final outcome of your pieces. Gas kilns allow you to fire in reduction. This is when the amount of oxygen within the kiln is reduced, which creates a carbon-rich atmosphere. This process can create very beautiful effects on the clay and glazes like speckles and very rich, earthy tones.

WOOD KILNS

Wood kilns have been used for thousands of years and come in a wide range of different shapes and sizes. They require constant supervision, graphing and reacting to the heat, and there is a lot of wood ash present which interacts with the glazes in the kiln.

RAKU FIRING

Raku firing is when the pot is removed from the heat of (usually) an electric kiln at around 900°C (1652°F) and generally plunged into a flammable material like newspaper or sawdust. Alternatively, materials like horsehair or feathers can be placed on the surface of the pot, which will burn away immediately but leave a carbon shadow of decoration. Raku firings can create very dramatic finishes but are not considered food-safe as they are not fired hot enough.

End

PIT FIRING

For this traditional method, a hole is dug in the ground lined with combustible materials. The pot is generally wrapped in flammable and reactive materials, such as copper wire, leaves and certain types of wood ash, and a fire is lit beneath the pots. During the process of the 'kiln' heating up and cooling down, these combustible materials burn and react with the pot. As with raku, items fired in this way are not considered food-safe.

HOW TO LOAD A KILN

Kilns are stacked so that layers of pieces can be loaded and fired at once. It is worth firing a completely full kiln as it is expensive to reach high temperatures, and firing a mostly empty kiln is very energy inefficient. Kiln shelves and props will help you make the most of the space: the props come in different heights and are like mini pillars that support the shelves.

1. Before you start loading, check where the thermocouple is and mind that you don't knock it with your shelves or pots.
2. On the very bottom of the kiln, place three small kiln props. Ensure they are evenly spread around the kiln, about 1–2cm (⅜–¾in) away from the wall, making sure to be clear of the line of the thermocouple. If you place four props, it will create a wobble: three is more stable. This shelf is to create airflow around the bottom of the kiln, as well as protecting the base of the kiln.
3. Place the first shelf on the props, making sure there is a gap between the kiln walls and the shelf. Place three more kiln props in line with the props below, making sure they are taller than the items you are going to add to this shelf. Keep all props lined up above one another to keep them structurally sound.
4. Place as many items as you can fit into the kiln, around the props. Never allow a piece to touch the elements or thermocouple. For a bisque firing, smaller items can be stacked inside other pieces. Cups, bowls and plates can be stacked rim to rim. Pieces can touch, as nothing is melting, but try not to stack too many things on top of flat or wide pieces, as pieces may crack when they aren't able to shrink freely. For a glaze firing, make sure there is at least 5mm (¼in) between each glazed item. When glaze melts, it will stick to anything it is touching.
5. Place another shelf on top of the props, ensuring none of the pots below are touching the base of the shelf. Ensure at least approximately 5mm (¼in) of space between the pots and the shelf above.
6. Continue adding shelves and pottery until you reach the top of the kiln. You do not need to place a shelf on the top layer. Ensure that there is enough room for the lid to close on the kiln.

Tips

- Take note of the thickness of the lid on a top-loader or the door of a front-loader. Some kilns will have bricks or insulation which can protrude into the kiln space when the lid or door is closed.
- Some glazes have high amounts of colourants which can give neighbouring pots a blush, when extra particles from the pigment are transferred onto the surface of a nearby pot. Take note of that when loading different coloured glazes next to each other.
- For the most efficient firing, try to keep layers of the kiln to similar heights. For example, load cups in one layer, plates and shorter pieces in the next, and the last layer can be tall vases or coffee pots. This ensures that the least amount of vertical space is wasted. This isn't always possible, but it should be the aim when stacking.
- Always let the kiln cool down to below 100°C (212°F) before opening it. This is to avoid thermal shock on the pots and the elements in the kiln. Pots will still be hot at this stage, however, so either wear gloves to unload the kiln or allow it to cool further until the pieces are cool enough to handle.
- Leave the kiln vented until it heats up to about 600°C (1112°F). After that, put the bung in and/or close the peepholes. This allows any organic material to burn off and moisture to leave the kiln.

BISQUE FIRING

A bisque firing for most clay is around 1000°C (1832°F). This firing is designed to fire off all the remaining moisture from the clay, as well as the water that is chemically bound within the clay.

Once a piece is out of the bisque firing, you'll notice that it has changed a lot. It shrinks, it changes colour, and it feels different too. It also behaves differently: it has become a little stronger and is incredibly porous. If you flick a drop of water onto the surface of bisqueware, you'll notice that it is very quickly wicked up by the ceramic. It acts like a sponge, and if you looked at it through a microscope, you'd see it looks similar – it has very open pores.

Bisqueware is usually a midpoint for ceramics. It's when you would glaze your work and then pop it back into the kiln for another firing to finish. Delightfully, a bisque firing is also known as a biscuit firing.

AN EXAMPLE OF A BISQUE FIRING PROGRAMME

The instructions for your clay may recommend a firing like the one here:

60°C (140°F) per hour to 600°C (1112°F)
100°C (212°F) per hour to 1000°C (1832°F)
15-minute soak

Modern kilns have controllers, which allow them to be programmed to a firing schedule like the one above. The slow initial ramp allows all moisture in the pieces to turn to steam slowly. Any faster and trapped steam can cause explosions – heartbreaking!

After 600°C (1112°F), the water is removed, and the programme can move a little bit faster. The 'soak' at the end of the programme refers to the kiln holding the same temperature for 15 minutes. This ensures that all the pieces reach the same temperature, not just the ones closest to the elements.

GLAZE FIRING

Once you have glazed your bisqueware, it goes back into the kiln and is fired to a higher temperature to melt the glaze. Glaze temperatures vary depending on the temperature of the clay that you have used (see the clay section on page 14).

When selecting your firing temperature, you must make sure that the kiln is hot enough for the clay and glaze to reach maturity (that is, the hottest possible firing temperature for each), but not so hot that the clay will bloat or melt. Check the firing range for your clay to ensure it is not going to be fired too hot – many kilns have been lost to earthenware melting in a stoneware firing!

The different ingredients in the glaze will melt at these high temperatures and the ceramic will shrink a little bit more. If you are using stoneware, this is when the clay becomes vitrified (watertight).

AN EXAMPLE STONEWARE GLAZE FIRING

The instructions for your glaze may recommend a firing like the one here:

150°C (302°F) per hour to 850°C (1562°F)
80°C (176°F) per hour to 1280°C (2336°F)
15-minute soak

This firing programme starts a lot faster than a bisque firing as there is very little steam to be removed from the pieces at this stage and the risk of explosion is far less. However, at around 800–900°C (1472–1652°F), the kiln may start to struggle to keep the high rate of heating, so slowing it down helps it get to the high temperature required. The soak is much the same as in a bisque firing in that it allows all of the pieces in the kiln to reach temperature and, in this case, it also allows the glaze to melt.

PROJECTS

PROJECTS

Welcome to part 3. Perhaps you found your way here after having a whole lot of practice from the front end of this book, or perhaps you jumped straight here, looking for inspiration for where to start. Either way, there are loads of projects outlined here with step-by-step instructions. They're split into beginner, intermediate and advanced levels, but they are all doable for many different levels, and some people will find some projects easier than others.

All these projects will need some throwing practice, so if you're not sure how to approach something, head back to the first part of the book for a reminder on how to throw a cylinder (see page 28) or a bowl (page 32). Detailed instructions for trimming cylinders can be found on page 44, and for making footrings see page 46.

All the pieces start by being centred and will finish with running a wooden knife tool along under the base and wiring the pot off.

SET OF MUGS

These are my favourite type of cups to make. I estimate that I've made thousands of these throughout my career so far. I love throwing a batch of cups or mugs and then making some handles, then sitting down with a podcast or a TV show on my computer and attaching the handles all in one go.

The point of this project is to get you throwing consistently, so throw a set of mugs with the goal of making them as identical as possible.

Materials and tools

Clay, approximately. 300–350g (10½–12½oz) per mug, plus around 50g (1¾oz) extra for a handle
Ruler
Throwing gauge (optional)
Cutting wire
Sponge and water

THROWING

1. Throw a cylinder following the instructions on page 28. You can make it straight up and down or shape it so it has a taper or a belly – whatever you like, as long as you can repeat it.
2. Measure the mug and note down its dimensions. If you have a throwing gauge, you can set this up to throw to the same measurements or you can use a ruler.
3. Repeat to make five more mugs, then leave them to dry until you can flip them upside down and trim them.
4. Before you begin trimming, make the handles so they can harden up a little. See pages 50–52 to make pulled or slab handles. I always make a few extras in case I make a mistake when attaching them. You don't want them to be properly leather hard, but you want them slightly firmer than fresh-out-of-the-bag clay.

TRIMMING

5. Trim your cups so that they all have identical bases (see page 40). If it's warm in your workspace, cover the cups when you're not working on them.

FINISHING

6. Attach your first handle (see page 53). I tend to attach a batch of six handles at a time, attaching them all first, and tidying afterwards. I find that this is faster than completing each handle individually, but see what works best for you.
7. Ensure that all the handles are the same shape.
8. Finish each mug with a sponge and, if it's warm in your workspace, drape some plastic over the top to ensure slow drying.

▲ FOR THE CUP ON THE LEFT TURN TO PAGE 56

RIDGE CUP

A ridge cup is a playful design which combines a cylinder and a bowl. I have added a little footring to mine for some added interest.

Shaping is the skill you'll be working on in this project. Concentrate on making slow, calm movements. You'll be using a wooden rib to get some nice, sharp angles, and it's important to think of the rib as an extension of your fingers.

I have placed this project in the beginner section, but it is on the trickier end. If you struggle with the shaping, keep practising. It will pay off in all future projects to learn how to control the clay effectively now.

Materials and tools

Clay, 250g (9oz)
Wooden rib
Teardrop and double-ended loop tools
Cutting wire
Sponge and water

THROWING

1. Centre the clay and throw a short cylinder (see page 28). Mine is 7cm (2¾in) high and 7cm (2¾in) wide.
2. On pulling up the wall for the last time, press outwards to bring the clay in a diagonal line for approximately 2cm (¾in), before repositioning your hands and bringing them upwards in a straight line.
3. Slowly remove your hands and inspect the cup. Sometimes, pulling the diagonal wall out will make the rim cone inwards. Reduce the wheel speed and refine the angle of the bottom edge by using the straight edge of your wooden rib tool. Hold your tool here for a few rotations of the wheel and then slowly remove the rib tool. Refine the vertical wall by holding the straight edge on the wall, but very slowly press your fingers on the inside of the cup against the edge of the rib. Remember that the rib is an extension of your hand here, so rather than holding it static while the wheel moves around, slowly move the rib up the wall of the clay, as you would when pulling.
4. Compress the rim one more time to recentre before wiring off and leaving it to dry to leather hard.

TRIMMING

5. Turn the pot upside down, centre it on the wheel head (see page 42) and attach it.
6. Using the teardrop trimming tool, flatten the base. If you'd like to add a footring (see page 46), carve out your guidelines with the square end loop tool and remove excess clay.
7. For the angled ridge, hold your loop tool at an angle until it is flattened and refined.
8. Rather than following the curve as on a bowl, remove your tool and repeat this hold on the vertical edge, if required.
9. Sponge the pot off, remove the pot from the wheel and sponge the rim to tidy it up. Leave to dry.

▼ STEP 1

▲ STEP 6

▼ STEP 3.1

▼ STEP 3.2

▲ STEP 7

▲ STEP 9

SAUCER

Now that you have the hang of different types of cup, why not graduate to a teacup with matching saucer? The teacup is really a tiny bowl with a handle added to it, but any cup will work with your saucer.

Materials and tools

Clay, 280g (10oz)
Bat
Ruler
Callipers or wooden knife tool
Teardrop and double-ended loop tools
Lugs
Cutting wire
Sponge and water

THROWING

1. Measure the base of your cup and note this down – if your cup has already been fired, you need to add your shrinkage to this measurement, usually somewhere around 10%.
2. Centre your clay on the bat and open it to a wide disk.
3. Once you have flattened the disk out, start pulling up a wall and scoop it outwards with the round of your sponge, as you would when making a wide bowl. Leave a thick enough base to trim out the depression for the cup to sit into plus an optional footring on the base.
4. Wire through the base and leave it to dry on the bat until it releases itself.

TRIMMING

5. Centre the saucer on the wheel head for trimming, but this time do it right-side up to begin with. Using a ruler and callipers or a wooden knife tool, mark the circumference measurement of the base of the cup on the saucer.
6. Using the square edge of the double-ended loop tool, carefully carve out this ring. Remove about 1–2mm (up to ⅛in) of clay to create the depression for the cup to sit in. Ensure it is flat, then sponge it off.
7. Turn the saucer over and trim the base. If your cup has a footring, it is a nice touch to add a footring to the saucer too, and if not, leave it flat.
8. Sponge it off and remove it from the wheel. Check that the cup fits before leaving the saucer to dry fully.

▼ STEP 2

▼ STEP 3.1

▲ STEP 6

▲ STEP 7.1

▼ STEP 3.2

▼ STEP 5

▲ STEP 7.2

▲ STEP 8

MILK JUG

This project is a practice of working with a different type of cylinder, as – this one is a cone shape. The shaping can be amended to suit your style, but I would like you to make this shape at least once to get the feel for it. Throwing a taper which goes inwards can be challenging – it's fighting against the forces of the wheel, and can be a little fiddly.

Materials and tools

Clay, 280g (10oz)
Sponge on a stick (just tie a sponge to the end of a stick if you don't have one of these)
Rib
Knife tool
Cutting wire
Lugs
Water

THROWING

1. Centre the clay and start making a cylinder.
2. While you are pulling up the clay, try to not let it flare outwards as you might with a cup but keep it in a cone shape. It helps if you visualize the cone shape you're making, and keep your hands aiming for that as you're pulling, and if you need to, you can collar the clay at the end of a pull to bring it back inwards (see page 37).
3. Once you have the clay at the height that you're after, get your sponge on a stick and mop up any excess water on the inside of the jug.
4. Use a rib to straighten the sides if you would like.
5. Use the wooden knife tool to create a chamfer on the base, and remove any water on the inside of the jug with a sponge on a stick.
6. To create the pouring lip, dip your finger and thumb into water and gently rub horizontally an area of around 1cm (3⁄8in) of the rim. This will thin the clay, so be careful not to rub through.
7. With one hand's thumb and forefinger, brace the outside of the wall around the thinned area. Pull your index finger of the opposite hand through the space between. This will pull the clay outwards and down.
8. This can make the rim a little less round, so gently press outwards to rectify this.
9. Wire through and remove the jug from the wheel and allow it to dry to leather hard.

▼ STEP 4

▼ STEP 5.1

▲ STEP 7

▲ STEP 11.1

▼ STEP 5.2

TRIMMING

10. Turn the jug upside down on the wheel, centre it, and secure to the wheelhead. Ensure that the lugs are not damaging the pulled lip.
11. Trim the base and the walls as you would a cylinder.
12. **Optional**: add a handle. As a milk jug typically doesn't hold hot liquid, it's not needed but can be added for decoration (see page 49).

▲ STEP 11.2

PLATE

A plate can easily become an advanced project if you size up. Start with smaller plates and graduate to larger sizes when you feel as though you can handle the weight of clay.

Note that plates have a bad reputation for warping and cracking, so if your first few don't make it, that's not on you!

Materials and tools

Clay, approximately 400g (14oz) for a small plate or 1200g (2½lb) or more for a large dinner plate
Totally flat bat
Wooden rib
Wooden knife tool
Needle tool
Teardrop and double-ended loop tools
Cutting wire
Sponge and water

THROWING

1. Start by prepping your wheel with a flat bat. If it's warped at all, that will make it difficult to throw the plate, and may lead to a warped finished piece.
2. Centre the clay, wide and flat.
3. From the very centre of the wheel, 'open' the clay by dragging it outwards and down simultaneously. You will need both hands to do this and it takes a lot of pressure.
4. Keep dragging the clay out until the clay is consistently around 1cm (⅜in) thick or even thicker if you want a footring.
5. Compress the clay by dragging your sponge from the middle down to 6 o'clock and back again a few times. Repeat with the flat side of the wooden rib to really get a really flat base.
6. To create a lip, dig the corner of your thumb under the edge of the plate, and fold this upwards: it is worth bracing your wrist with your other hand here.
7. Shape the wall – you may want a 90° angle, or something more curved. Tidy the wall with a wooden knife tool, and use a needle tool to cut the rim off to ensure it is flat (see page 36).
8. Drag your wooden knife tool under the base to create a channel for the wire.
9. Ensure your wire is held very taut, and drag it through the base, pressing down very firmly – when wiring wide pieces, it's easy for any slack in the wire to cut right through the base.

▼ STEP 2

▼ STEP 3

▲ STEP 7

▲ STEP 13

▼ STEP 5

▲ STEP 14

Tips

- It can be difficult to get the very centre of the plate looking nice and flat, and it's very easy for tools to gouge the middle out. Sometimes the best tool for this is a sponge, but I find that using the curved edge of a wooden rib slightly overlapping the very centre of the plate creates a smooth finish.
- With large pieces, it may help to have the wheel turning very slowly while you wire off. This usually helps if you find it difficult to wire all the way though and it also helps with releasing the plate later.

TRIMMING

10. Once the plate is leather hard, it should release itself from the bat. Sometimes wider plates can be stubborn and may require coaxing with a wire, or by flipping the whole thing over and peeling the bat off bit by bit. Note that the middle may get stuck, so as soon as the bat starts releasing, you can kind of twist it, so that it doesn't pull the stuck bits with it.
11. Place the plate upside down on the wheel head and stick it down (see page 42).
12. If you want a footring, draw your guides in and remove the excess clay. Note that if your plate is particularly wide, you may need two footrings – one close to the middle, and one on the outside – so that the middle doesn't sag in the kiln and stick to the shelf.
13. I don't tend to give my plates footrings, so I make sure to flatten the base off and give it a 45° angle chamfer, like my cylinders.
14. After trimming, sponge the plate off and leave it to dry on a very flat surface – very slowly.

SOAP DISH

A soap dish is a lovely project that can be quite adaptable. I make the same shape for snack and soap dishes, as well as spoon rests (I just chop the side off!).

This is the same shape as the plate we made on page 90, just a lot smaller. I make my soap dishes a little thicker on the base as I need to give them a footring for water drainage. Throw this project on a bat.

Materials and tools

Clay, 300g (10½oz)
Wooden bat
Needle tool
Wooden rib
Lugs
Teardrop and double-ended loop tools
Knife tool
Hole cutter if you have one, or a drill bit approximately 5mm (¼in) wide
Cutting wire
Sponge and water

THROWING

1. Centre the clay wide and flat on a bat.
2. Bring the clay out until the base is approximately 1.5cm (⅝in) thick: check this with a needle tool (see the tip below).
3. Bring the walls of the soap dish up by pressing your thumb into the clay where it meets the bat. Firmly press inwards, and the rim will fold upwards.
4. Tidy up the wall with the flat edge of the wooden rib and trim the rim off if it's wobbly (see page 36).
5. Finish as usual, and wire through the base, but then leave the soap dish to dry on the bat.

TRIMMING AND FINISHING

6. Place the soap dish upside down on the wheel head, centre and secure to the wheel head (see page 42).
7. Flatten the base with a loop tool. Create a chamfer where the base and the wall meet, and then carve a line for an internal footring (see page 46).
8. Cut in the internal footring, ensuring it is nice and flat.
9. With the wheel still slowly spinning, hold a needle tool approximately 5mm (¼in) from the centre of the soap dish and gently draw a faint line. Repeat this around 1cm (⅜in) away from this first line.

10. Stop the wheel spinning, and draw a faint straight line across the circles – you will cut your holes where the circles and the line cross. Remove the soap dish from the wheel.
11. Using a hole cutter or drill bit, cut three holes through the base of the soap dish. I also carve a little divot through my footring to allow water to drain out.
12. Using a very lightly damp sponge, wipe away the drawn lines and any marks left from trimming or cutting holes.

Tip

- If you're having trouble gauging how thick your base is, you can place a needle tool all the way into the base until it reaches the bat or the wheel head. With your finger, mark where the clay meets the needle. As you remove the tool from the base, your finger will show you the depth of your base.

▼ STEP 1

▲ STEP 11.1

▼ STEP 3

▼ STEP 7

▲ STEP 11.2

▲ STEP 12

WIDE SHALLOW BOWL

This style of bowl may well be my best seller. It's a favourite of mine, too, because it functions as both a plate and a bowl. It can be challenging to make, however, because the clay can very easily flop when it is being pushed outwards. Take care to leave enough clay on the base to support the shoulder.

Materials and tools

Clay, 1000-1200g (2¼–2½lb), although if you are having trouble with the shape, start smaller, with 600-800g (1¼–1¾lb) and work up to a larger amount of clay when the movements have been honed
Wooden bat
Teardrop and double-ended loop tools
Cutting wire
Sponge and water

THROWING

1. Centre the clay, wide and flat, using a wooden bat.
2. Follow the instructions for throwing a bowl on page 32. Be mindful that although this bowl is not very tall, it's important to get enough height before you begin pressing the clay out. Ensure you follow the shape of the bowl as you pull up the walls, following the scooping motion.
3. Once the walls are high enough (generally aim 2–3cm (about 1in) higher than you'd like to finish with), start shaping your bowl. Press the clay out wide, starting right at the base of the pot. Ensure your hands are working in unison as you coax the clay outwards until a generous width has been established, 2–3cm (about 1in) wider than the base.
4. To keep a round shape, slowly change the direction of your hands to follow the curve of the bowl. Think about a scooping motion – out, and then up. This will stop it flaring all the way out. If you would like a straight wall, which diagonally flares outwards, don't change direction when pulling. It's important that the shoulder has enough clay beneath it for the pot to stay upright because if it is unsupported, it will succumb to gravity and flop. You can trim excess clay later.

▼ STEP 1

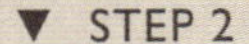

▼ STEP 2

▲ STEP 9.1

▲ STEP 9.2

▼ STEP 4

▲ STEP 9.3

5. Finish the bowl as usual, and wire through the base. Leave it on the bat to dry until leather hard.

6. There is likely to be a lot of clay on the base that needs to harden. You may need to wrap a little plastic around the rim of the bowl when it gets to leather hard to allow the base to catch up. Sometimes I will cut the bowl off the bat when it has hardened a little so that I can flip the bowl upside down to dry.

TRIMMING

7. Once the base of the bowl is leather hard, measure the depth of the base following instructions on page 40.

8. Attach the bowl upside down to the wheelhead.

9. Follow the steps on page 46 to trim in a footring. Keep around 0.5–1cm (¼–⅜in) of width at the base of the bowl to ensure it doesn't crack, and make sure that the footring is wide enough to support the width of the bowl as well – you don't want it tipping over when it's full of soup! Generally, start with the wider part of the footring being around half of the diameter of the rim of the bowl. This is a very rough guide, and you can amend this, but it's a good starting point.

10. Finish your bowl with a lightly dampened sponge and let it dry slowly.

This project can be used to create very large bowls of the same design – just add more clay slowly. Note that the wider you go, the wider the centred base of clay will need to be when you are opening.

PORRIDGE BOWL

Like the previous bowl, this one can be amended to be as large or as small as you wish. These bowls are great for porridge and for soupy things like ramen or curry. I like my porridge bowls to have a really substantial footring so that they can be held by the foot if the walls are too hot.

Materials and tools

Clay, 800-1200g (1¾–2½lb), depending on the size you would like
Wooden bat
Wooden knife tool
Wooden rib
Teardrop and double-ended loop tools
Needle tool
Cutting wire
Round sponge and water

THROWING

1. Centre the clay, wide.
2. Follow the instructions on page 32 to throw a bowl.
3. When pulling up the walls, ensure that you achieve at least the height you want before pushing the clay outwards. Keep the walls thick enough to be able to be pressed out without flopping.
4. When the walls have been pulled up, it's time to widen. I like my porridge bowls to be very round, so I keep a close eye on my mirror as I am shaping. With a round sponge, and a slow wheel speed, press outwards with your left hand on the inside of the bowl, and support the clay on the outside with your right hand.
5. Allow a curve to form when shaping by repeating the scooping motion as mentioned in the steps on page 98.
6. Follow the curve all the way to the top of the bowl and ensure that you compress the rim to keep it nice and sturdy.
7. Finish the pot off as usual and wire through the base. Leave it on the bat to dry until leather hard.
8. There is likely to be a lot of clay on the base that needs to harden. You may need to wrap a little plastic around the rim of the bowl when it gets to leather hard to allow the base to catch up. Sometimes I will cut the bowl off the bat when it has hardened a little so that I can flip the bowl upside down to dry.

TRIMMING

9. Once the base of the bowl is leather hard, measure the depth of the base following the instructions on page 40.
10. Attach the bowl upside down to the wheelhead.
11. Follow the steps on page 46 to cut in a footring. Keep around 0.5–1cm (¼–⅜in) of width at the base of the bowl to ensure it doesn't crack.
12. Try to match the shape of the outside of the bowl to the inside. You will trim a lot of clay off the shoulder, and sometimes I find that my tool can start wobbling on the surface of these larger bowls. To stop this, ensure you hold your trimming tool very tightly with both hands. Keep your tool still – let it trim the topmost part of the bowl on each rotation of the wheel. As the wobble is trimmed away, the surface of the bowl will become more even.
13. Finish your bowl with a lightly dampened sponge and let it dry slowly.

This project can be used to create very large bowls of the same design – just add more clay slowly. Note that the wider you go, the wider the centred base of clay will need to be when you are opening.

▼ STEP 3

▲ STEP 6

▼ STEP 4

▼ STEP 5

▲ STEP 11

▲ STEP 12

CUSTARD JUG

This crazy jug looks a little more ornate within my collection of work. I have included it as a project to show that you can achieve really cool finishes with your pieces if you do a little amending. I cut half of the rim of this jug to get the shape of the lip.

You may want to use a bat for this project.

Materials and tools

Clay, 700g (1½lb)
Wooden rib tool
Needle tool
Knife tool
Loop tools if you are going to add a footring
Pencil or paintbrush
Cutting wire
Sponge and water

THROWING

1. Centre the clay. Throw a tall cylinder following the instructions on page 28.
2. Create a belly in the jug by pressing outwards, and then scooping back in. To help with proportions, think about the halfway point, and the two-thirds point. Start bellying out to the halfway point, and then bring the clay back in towards the two thirds point. You can collar in at the top (see page 37) to help emphasize the belly shape. Repeat this step if you want the belly to be a little wider.
3. Next, flare the top third out to create the rim. Ideally, this shouldn't be wider than the belly of the pot to keep it looking in proportion.
4. Refine everything with a wooden rib tool, finish the pot off as usual and cut it off the wheel.

TRIMMING AND FINISHING

5. Make a handle following the steps on pages 50–52. I made a slab handle, shaped it around a rolling pin and placed it aside on a board. However, a pulled handle would also look great on this style of piece. Leave the handle aside as you're trimming to harden up a little.
6. When the jug is leather hard, turn it upside down and trim it, following the instructions on page 44. Adding a footring is optional for this project.
7. After trimming, turn the jug the right way up, and place a flat tool across the diameter of the rim to find the halfway points. Mark these points, one at the top of the rim and one where the flange starts to flare out.

▼ STEP 2

▼ STEP 2.1

▲ STEP 7

▲ STEP 10

▼ STEP 4

▲ STEP 12

8. At the top point, measure 1–2cm (3/8–3/4in) each side and mark. This will be the lip, so if you would like it larger or smaller, mark this either side of the midpoint. Note that it's much easier to start bigger – you can always trim a little more off later but it's a lot more difficult to add more on!
9. With a needle tool, gently draw a diagonal line from the bottom point up towards the spout points on the inside of the flange. Repeat this on the other side.
10. With a knife tool, carefully cut along your diagonal lines. You may need to even up the rim a little with the knife tool. Once the rim looks even, tidy the cut marks with a damp sponge.
11. Wet your thumb and index finger and rub the lip while gently pinching. This will thin the rim out a little and soften the clay.
12. With one hand's thumb and forefinger, brace the outside of the wall around the thinned area. Pull your index finger of the opposite hand through the space between. This will pull the clay outwards and down. You may need to repeat this a couple of times to get the shape you need, but be careful not to split the lip.
13. Add the handle following the steps on page 53.
14. Finish everything off with a lightly dampened sponge.

EGG CUPS OFF THE HUMP

This project is designed to show a cool skill – throwing off the hump! Throwing tiny things like egg cups can be tricky. Centring less than 150g (5¼oz) of clay can be really difficult as there is so little clay compared to the size of our hands. To get around this, you can throw off the hump! This is when you roughly centre a large piece of clay and use only the top portion of it to make your pot. Then when you're done, you cut it off, and start a new one right where you left off.

I don't tend to measure my clay when throwing off the hump, but you need enough clay to make multiple pieces. Use the amount of clay that you are comfortable throwing. You might find that somewhere around 1000–2000g (2¼–4½lbs) works well.

I am making egg cups for this project, but you can use this technique for any type of smaller piece. Some people make quite substantial sized pots off the hump – it just takes practice! Once you get the hang of it, this technique can be really efficient.

Tips

- It's harder to judge how thick your base is when throwing off the hump as there is no wheel head to measure against. It's better to cut it off slightly thicker than you think, rather than thinner, as you can trim off any excess later.
- Cutting pieces off the hump can be fiddly. I find it's easiest to carve a channel for the wire to go through with a wooden knife tool and then cut it off with the wire when the wheel is spinning very slowly. If you leave a big base, you can pick your piece up from there without damaging the rim.
- You will naturally be positioned a little higher at the wheel than you're used to. Make sure to anchor your elbows into your ribs and hinge forward at the hips to stay stable. You may be used to being anchored to the splash pan or your legs.

Materials and tools

Clay, approximately 1000–2000g (2¼–4½lbs) works well
Water and sponge
Wooden knife tool
Cutting wire

▼ STEP 1

▼ STEP 3.1

▲ STEP 5.1

▲ STEP 5.2

▼ STEP 3.2

▲ STEP 6

THROWING

1. Roughly centre a large mound of clay. When throwing larger pieces, you can start by slapping the clay into place on the wheel as it is moving very slowly. Then when you start the centring proper, really use the weight of your body to help you get the clay where you want it to be. Be patient with it – it takes longer to move so much clay into the middle!
2. The most important thing when throwing off the hump is to have the piece of clay that you're working on properly centred (see page 26). The rest can be ignored, but having it mostly centred will help.
3. Make a little shelf of clay to visualize where the base of the pot is going to be. From there, throw your egg cup as you would a small bowl: opening, pulling up the walls and shaping.
4. Throw your egg-cup shape and measure it. Generally, an egg cup is around 4–5cm (1½–2in) in diameter, so ensure you add your shrinkage rate to your final measurements. For more on shrinkage, go to page 17.
5. Leave a thick-enough base and then create a channel under your egg cup with your wooden knife tool with a generous base. Guide your wire through, holding it very taut, and slow the wheel speed right down. Keep your hands as level as possible as you do this.
6. Stop the wheel and, using the thick base, remove the egg cup from the hump and then place it on a board to dry.
7. Recentre the clay at the top of the hump where you left off and repeat the process until no clay is left.

TRIMMING

8. Trim your egg cups the same way you would a cylinder or a bowl. You will find that there is a lot of base to trim off, so go slow and be patient.

Practice makes perfect with these!

COLANDER

I first made a colander as a little berry dish. I was at my parents' house in New Zealand, picking strawberries and popping them into a little bucket, and we walked them inside to wash them and then put them in a bowl. I thought that a nice gift for them would be a berry bowl that doubled as a colander to save effort.

Later, I upsized the berry bowl into a small and a large colander, and I now use one at home to drain my pasta!

Materials and tools

Clay, 1000-1200g (2¼–2½lb) for a large colander – use more or less clay to size up or down
Wooden bat
Needle tool
Teardrop and double-ended loop tools
Hole cutter or drill bit
Pencil or paintbrush
Cutting wire
Sponge and water

THROWING AND TRIMMING

1. Follow the steps on page 98 to throw a wide shallow bowl and trim a footring into it (see page 46). This is my favourite shape of bowl for this project, although any bowl will work!

FINISHING

2. Once you have trimmed in a footring, leave the bowl in place on the wheel. Using a needle tool, lightly trace two circles, one in the very centre of the bowl, and one around 1cm (⅜in) away on the inside of the footring. Stop the wheel, and divide these circles up like a pizza – lightly draw a line through the middle of the centre circle out to the next, and then draw two more, evenly spaced around.

3. With the wheel slowly spinning again, draw three or four more horizontal lines, evenly spaced, on the body of the bowl. Don't draw a line within approximately 1cm (⅜in) of the rim to ensure it doesn't crack.

4. Stop the wheel. Following the lines drawn on the inside of the circle, draw vertical lines on the body of the bowl. I also add a line in between each line from the footring holes – they seem too sparse on the body without. Where these horizontal and vertical lines intercept is where you will cut your holes in the colander.

5. Unstick your bowl from the wheel head, but keep it upside down.

6. With a hole cutter or drill bit, cut the very middle hole out, and the six holes inside the footring.
7. Following the lines on the body of the bowl, cut holes in the body of the bowl. Depending on how many holes you would like, you may want to add holes in between the areas marked, too.
8. Once all the holes have been cut, wring out your sponge and remove the drawn lines. Do this by rubbing your sponge in circles over the lines. Re-dip your sponge and wring it out from time to time. Be wary not to add too much water, as this will weaken the pot.
9. Flip your colander over and remove any clay crumbs from the hole cutting – you can scrape these off with a loop tool. Clean up the inside with a sponge.

ADDING OPTIONAL HANDLES

10. If you wish to add handles, follow the instructions on pages 50–52 and make two small handles, either slab-shaped or pulled.
11. Using a paintbrush, or a tool that can span the diameter of the colander, mark the two halfway points – make sure that where you would like your handles to attach to the body is not over a hole.
12. Trim your handle ends to fit the form of the colander. Mine end up at around a 45° angle.
13. Follow instructions on page 53 to attach your handles.

▼ STEP 2

▲ STEP 11

▼ STEP 7

▼ STEP 8

▲ STEP 12

▲ STEP 13

LEMON JUICER

Throwing a lemon juicer is so joyous. It feels out of control and a little bit silly until suddenly it's done! It's a slightly different technique to everything else in so far as it starts with throwing a donut shape.

Give it a few goes if you can't quite work out the ratios of clay to leave for the middle and for the outside. I recommend throwing this piece on a bat.

This piece uses a chuck for trimming. To throw a chuck, find instructions on page 48.

Materials and tools

Clay, 600g (1¼lb)
Bat
Leather-hard chuck
Wooden knife tool
Rib
Needle tool
Loop tools
Cutting wire
Sponge and water

THROWING

1. Centre the clay on the bat as a wide puck shape. Then open the clay in the middle, right to the base of the bat, creating a donut.
2. Create a channel approximately 1cm (⅜in) away from the opening by pressing a finger or thumb into the clay. This should be around 1.5–2cm (⅝–¾in) deep, although this can be refined later.
3. Create the cone by pulling up clay from the middle of the donut. You want to get as much clay from the base as you can here, so you may wish to widen the opening to around 3cm (1¼in) as you pull up the clay. While you're pulling, aim the wall to the centre point.
4. Collar the clay gently to create the cone shape. Repeat until you have an enclosed cone.
5. Once you have the cone shape, the air enclosed within the clay will support it somewhat, so you can take a rib and shape the cone if you need to. Try to keep a pointy top if you can.
6. Now that the cone has been thrown, the channel can be tidied up. Pull the clay up a little on the sides to hold the juice that will flow into it, and tidy the rim.
7. Finish the pot as usual and wire it off the bat.
8. To create the pouring lip, dip your finger and thumb into water and gently rub an area of the rim of around 2cm (¾in). This will thin the clay, so be careful not to rub through.
9. With your opposite hand's thumb and forefinger, brace the outside of the wall around the thinned area, and bring your finger through the space between. The action can be repeated if required, but the thinned clay may split if it's handled too much.
10. Leave the juicer to dry to leather hard.

▼ STEP 1

▼ STEP 3

▲ STEP 13

▲ STEP 15

▼ STEP 5

▲ STEP 16

Tips

- Pulling the cone up will feel very strange compared to other pots that you've thrown – usually the inside fingers lean on the base of clay, and the outside fingers are on the wheel head. It's reversed here, so take your time and be patient if it doesn't quite work the first time.
- Try to sponge up the water on the inside of the cone before it's closed, but don't worry if you're not able to. As the cone doesn't have clay on the bottom, it's not as likely to crack from excess water.
- You can blow into the cone before you close it. This will puff up the shape a little bit. Make sure you wipe your mouth and don't swallow the clay though!

TRIMMING

11. Centre and stick your chuck to the wheel, following the instructions on page 42.
12. Dip your finger in water and wet the rim of the leather-hard chuck. Then place the juicer upside down on the chuck. Once it's centred, gently tap its base to get it to stick to the rim of the chuck.
13. Trim excess clay from the base and tidy up the area where the cone meets the base. If you feel as though the cone is particularly thick, you can trim the inside of it now, although this is not necessary. You can trim the walls too, but be wary of damaging the lip if you added one in the throwing section.
14. Sponge your lemon juicer down and remove it from the chuck by gently lifting it off. It should unstick itself easily.

FINISHING

15. Add grooves to the cone of your juicer by scoring it with the corner of the square ended loop tool (although many different tools work here, and it is a good idea to experiment).
16. Once you have added the grooves, wring a sponge out and tidy up the cuts and any marks left by the chuck.

VASE

The last project of the intermediate section plays with form and surface decoration. Making it will help you practice the collaring technique and develop your ability to defy gravity a little bit with the flat flange. Make vases in a variety of sizes to create a little family of them.

Materials and tools

Clay, 700g (1½lb) or more
Bat
Wooden rib
Lugs
Loop tools to cut in the footring
Cutting wire
Sponge and water
Oxides, slip or coloured glaze to decorate plus appropriate brushes

THROWING

1. Centre the clay.
2. Throw a tall cylinder following the instructions on page 28. When pulling up the walls, ensure that the rim stays thick and sturdy – around 1cm (⅜in) thick. I like a stepped footring for this project, so I ensure that it's there when I am throwing. I do this by pulling the clay for the walls not from the very base of the wheel head, but from 1–2cm (⅜–¾in) higher than the base.
3. As with the custard jug, shaping is key here. Create a belly in the vase by pressing outwards, and then scooping back in. Your hands should be working in unison on each side of the vase wall – if you want to belly out, your inside hand will be pressing and your outside hand following along and supporting.
4. Once you have pressed the belly out, follow the top third of the clay upwards. Collar in the neck of the jar (see page 37). Go very slowly – if there are thin spots in the shoulder, the pot may collapse at this point!
5. Once you have collared in to a point you are happy with, pull the rim out a little more. Do this with the same technique as when pulling up a wall, but angle your hands outwards. It may feel a little weird, and this is also a point where your pot may collapse, so take it very slowly.
6. Refine everything with a wooden rib tool, especially the flange. Carefully press the flat edge of the wooden rib into the flange to tidy it all up. Don't forget to tidy the stepped footring, too, if you have thrown one in.
7. Finish the pot in the usual way and cut it off the wheel.

Tip

- To help with proportions, think about the halfway point, and the two-thirds point. Start bellying out to the halfway point, and then bring the clay back in towards the two thirds point. You can collar in at the top to help emphasize the belly shape. Repeat this step if you want the belly to be a little wider.

TRIMMING AND FINISHING

8. When the vase is leather hard, turn it upside down, centre it, and attach it to the wheel head with lugs. Note that the flange is very delicate and holding a lot of weight so if you over-wet it or knock the vase at this stage, you can very easily tear the flange off.
9. Adding a footring is optional for this project, although if you have thrown a stepped vase, it makes sense to add one. Use instructions on page 46 to add a footring.
10. After trimming and tidying with a sponge, remove your vase from the wheel and turn it the right way up.
11. If you are decorating your vase with slip or oxide, apply this now. Before painting, ensure the vase is fully sponged and looking good, and place it on a bat. This means you don't need to pick it up when drying, smudging your paint. I used a flat, wide glaze brush to apply mine – a mix of red iron oxide and water.

▼ STEP 1

▲ STEP 5

▼ STEP 2

▼ STEP 3

▲ STEP 9

▲ STEP 11

CANDLESTICK

I love this project – it's a special one for me. I made candlesticks as table decorations at my wedding and gave them to our guests as favours. They are tricky to make, so be patient with yourself and prepare to fail a few times. You'll eventually get the knack. This project uses similar techniques to the lemon juicer, so if you're really struggling with this one, go back to page 118 and work on that project first. It will help.

Ensure you know the shrinkage rate of your clay and the measurement of your candle before starting. Add your shrinkage to this measurement. Alternatively, you can use tapered table candles which you can press into the candlestick.

I use a set of tiny callipers for this project, set to the measurement I need. If you don't have this tool, just use a ruler.

Materials and tools

Clay, 250–400g (9–14oz)
Bat
Wooden knife tool (optional)
Ruler or callipers
Chuck
Cutting wire
Sponge and water

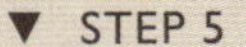

▼ STEP 4

▼ STEP 5

▲ STEP 7

▲ STEP 9

THROWING

1. Centre a ball of clay on a bat.
2. Separate a small section of clay to be the little bowl at the base of the centred clay by pressing in and down towards the bat, making a small pad of clay. Ignore it for now – we will refine it later.
3. With the remaining clay, open up to the wheel head.
4. Throw a tall, narrow cylinder (see page 28). Keep it narrow and cone-shaped as you pull up the walls, and try to avoid any thin spots!
5. Once you have pulled the clay up to around 10cm (4in), start to shape the candlestick. With your index finger and thumb of both hands, gently collar (see page 37) around the base to create a ridge. Repeat this motion just above it to create a second ridge.
6. Press the clay on the tall part of the cylinder up and out into a flange.
7. **Optional:** with a wooden knife tool, gently press the end into the top of the flange, creating a lip to hold the candle. This step is optional, because the candle will still fit into the candlestick with just the flange. The lip is more for decoration than anything.
8. Refine the base pad by pressing it out and pulling up a small wall to create a shallow bowl.
9. Check the measurement of the hole for the candle – you can press out slightly or collar in gently if needed.
10. Clean up with a sponge, create a chamfer under the base, and wire through. Lift the bat off the wheel and allow the candlestick to dry to leather hard.

Tips

- I suggest making the hole go all the way through to the wheel head, making a tube rather than keeping it enclosed. If you let the candle melt down too far, it's really difficult to get it out when enclosed, but the tube shape will allow the candle to be pushed through if needed.
- Shaping your candlestick may slightly push the top off centre, making it wobble a little. Try to steady this by compressing the rim lightly. If the wobble doesn't go away, you may still be able to work with the top, but you may lose it entirely. This happens – try again!

TRIMMING

11. Centre and secure your chuck (see page 48) to the wheel head. Lightly wet the rim of the chuck.
12. Place the leather-hard candlestick upside down on the chuck and centre. Press it down gently to secure it.
13. Flatten the base of the candlestick and tidy the walls of the bowl.
14. Tidy the middle area where the tube of the candlestick and base meet.
15. Sponge it all off and remove it from the chuck.

Tip

- If you'd like to refine the shape of the candlestick once it's leather hard, it's very possible to trim it down a little. Do this before steps 11–15 by securing it directly to the wheel head with some small lugs. Once you have refined it, then trim the base.

TEAPOT

A teapot feels like an item you simply have to make when taking up pottery – it's like a rite of passage! Teapots can have many forms. This is my take on one, but please do feel free to play with different forms, such as round or more triangular bodies, adding a knob to the lid, handles on the top rather than the side, or making the handles from a different material altogether – there are so many variations and possibilities.

The throwing is done in four units: body, spout, lid and handle. The clay weights in the materials list are approximate and can vary to fit different designs.

Materials and tools

Clay, 800g (1¾lb) for the body, 400g (14oz) for the spout, 200g (7oz) for the lid and 100g (3½oz) for the handle
Bat
Wooden rib
Callipers or ruler
Wooden knife tool
Needle tool
Loop tools
Cutting wire
Sponge and water

THROWING

Teapot body

1. Centre your clay on a bat.
2. Open up wide and start bringing the clay up into a cylinder. Keep the walls reasonably thick – the rim should stay around 1cm (⅜in) thick.
3. Once the walls have been pulled, it's time to create the flange. Hold the rim gently with your left hand and support the inside rim with your right hand. Fold the top 2.5cm (1in) or so down into your left hand, very slowly. Keep the flange at about a 45° angle.
4. Folding the flange may make the top of the walls flare out a little. Fix this by collaring back in (see page 37) while supporting the inside flange.
5. Flatten the body up with a wooden rib tool. Once this is complete, gently do the same on the flange. Guide the flange to a 90° angle with the rib. Always support the inside as you are doing this as it can easily flop.
6. If needed, use the rib again on the walls of the teapot.
7. Measure the diameter of the teapot opening as a guide for making the lid. Do this with a ruler or callipers.
8. Clean up with a sponge, create a chamfer under the base, and wire through. Lift the bat off the wheel and allow the pot to dry to leather hard.

▼ STEP 2

▼ STEP 3

▲ STEP 7

▲ STEP 10

▼ STEP 5.1

▼ STEP 5.2

▲ STEP 11

▲ STEP 13

▼ STEP 14

▼ STEP 15

▲ STEP 18

Lid

There are many different ways to throw a lid. This is my preferred way. You can also throw off the hump, right way up, and trim out the gallery afterwards. I tend to make one or two extra lids for a teapot and then choose the best one during the trimming process.

9. Place a bat on the wheel, and centre the clay, wide and flat.
10. Begin pinching some of the clay from the base upwards into a flange. Pull this clay up into a wall 2–3cm (about 1) in tall.
11. Measure with your callipers or ruler to make sure that it is narrow enough to fit into the opening on the teapot, without being so narrow that it will fall as you are pouring tea! This can be trimmed down to fit properly once it is leather hard, so just get the approximate size now.
12. Tidy up the whole lid with a sponge and then wire it off the bat. Lift the bat off and leave the lid to dry.

Spout

The spout is thrown off the hump. As with the lid, I tend to make a few and then choose the best one when assembling. I make a few different shapes – tall and narrow or short and stout. It's also nice to have a couple of back-ups in case the first one is damaged, as with the handles. Spouts will dry at a much faster rate than the body and lid of the teapot, so keep an eye on them and wrap them in plastic when they get to leather hard.

13. Roughly centre a mound of clay. Make a little shelf of clay to help visualize where the base of the spout is going to be. From there, throw a cone of clay. The rim should be reasonably thin – around 3mm (⅛in).
14. If you want, remove throwing lines with a wooden rib tool.
15. Channel under your spout with your wooden knife tool. Guide your wire through, hold it very taut, and slow the wheel speed right down. Carefully guide your wire through as the wheel is still spinning, keeping your hands as level as possible.
16. Stop the wheel and, picking it up by the base, remove the spout from the hump and place it on a board to dry.
17. Recentre the clay at the top of the hump where you left off, then repeat the process.
18. Once your spouts are all made, pull a tiny little pouring lip into them. This will make sure that the teapot will pour properly (the potter's dream!), without drips or dribbles. With one hand's thumb and forefinger, brace the outside of the wall. Dip the pinkie finger of your opposite hand in water and, very gently, pull it through the space between index finger and thumb. This will pull the clay outwards and down.

Handle

On the day of trimming, I tend to make a few handles first-thing. Handles take a lot less time to dry than thrown pieces – so doing it on trimming day allows them to dry to leather hard whilst everything else is being trimmed.

19. Make a couple of handles following the instructions on pages 50–52. I have made a slab handle for my teapot, but a pulled handle will also work.

Leave everything to get leather hard before moving on to the next steps. The body of the teapot may need to be cut off the bat at the leather-hard stage and turned over to allow the base to dry enough.

TRIMMING AND FINISHING

Body

20. Centre and secure the body of the teapot upside down on the wheel head (see page 42).
21. Trim off any excess on the base and walls using instructions on page 44. I just added a chamfer to my teapot, however you can add a footring (see page 46) if you'd like.
22. Sponge the piece down and remove it from the wheel.

Lid

23. Place the lid inside the teapot. If it's too tight and doesn't quite fit, measure the opening and note this down.

24. Cover the body of the teapot in plastic to prevent it from drying out while you work on the lid.

25. Attach the lid, flat-side down, to the wheel. Trim the flange down to the required size. Make sure that there's a gap between the flange and the opening of at least a few millimetres (⅛in). If it's too snug, it may not fit once it has been glazed.

26. Trim your lid down so the thickness of the lip and the base is about 5mm (¼in). Sponge it down to tidy it up and then remove it from the wheel. Check it fits and repeat steps 25 and 26 if it doesn't.

27. Tidy the top of the lid by either attaching it to the wheel head and trimming off any excess, or simply by sponging. Wrap the lid in plastic and set aside.

Spout

28. Select the spout that you think is the best looking and best shape for your teapot.

29. Cut the base off the thrown spout at approximately 60° with a knife tool. Trace around the spout before you cut so you know that it's even. Ensure that the wall with the pouring lip of the spout is the long side, and the opposite is short.

30. Shape the inside of the spout so that it will sit flush to the body of the teapot. I do this by gently rolling the round handle of any tool into the spout.

31. Hold it up to the teapot, and check that it looks good. If it looks as if the angle is wrong, amend this by trimming a little more off or rounding it a little more.

32. Once the spout is sitting flush, hold it where it will be placed and, using a needle tool, trace around both the inside and the outside of the spout onto the body.

33. Cut some holes in the inside ring, and tidy these up on both the inside and outside of the wall. Then score the inside of the ring and the edge of the spout.

34. Generously apply slip to the spout and firmly press it onto the body. Support the inside wall as you do this to ensure it does not misshape the teapot.

35. Tidy the join with a wooden knife tool and, if needed, roll a coil to help reinforce the join.

Handle

36. Once the handle has dried to leather hard, attach it following the instructions on page 53.

37. I attached my handle to the wall of the teapot, but many teapots have handles attached to the top. If you would like to have it on the top, do make sure that the lid can be used properly before attaching it.

38. Drape some plastic over top to let the teapot dry slowly. There are a lot of joins that may crack if it dries unevenly.

Tips

- Ensure the end of your teapot's spout is always higher than the internal waterline. If it's placed too low, you won't be able to fill up your teapot without it spilling!
- Ensure your handle is robust enough to hold both the weight of the pot and the weight of tea or coffee when it's filled.
- When glazing the teapot, make sure to scrape any glaze out of the holes in the spout before firing.
- Traditionally, a lid is fired on top of the teapot to ensure that it shrinks at the same rate as the body. This would mean that the gallery that the lid sits in must be unglazed, as well as the inner lip of the lid – otherwise the lid will stick. As I don't make a gallery for my lid to sit in, I break the rules here and I fire the lid and body separately. I wipe the base of the flange free of glaze and sit it next to the body in the firing. Try both ways to see which method you prefer.

▼ STEP 26

▼ STEP 29

▲ STEP 32

▲ STEP 34

LAMPSHADE

Creating a ceramic lampshade is a fun project, and there are many different things to consider. For example, what type of clay would you like to use? Porcelain would work very well because when it is thrown thin enough, it fires translucent. I used a red terracotta for my lampshade as I wanted a moody, directional light. Glaze is something to consider, too – using a white glaze would make for a more reflective lampshade, while something darker will absorb more light.

Form also needs to be considered. It's not just the shape of the lampshade that you're playing with here, but shadows and reflections as well. Start by drawing a few lampshade shapes to get an idea of what you would like to make.

If you don't have a specific light you are making this for, you can purchase plug-in lamp cords. Measure the fitting for the lampshade and make sure that you calculate shrinkage before you throw and trim your piece to ensure it fits.

Materials and tools

Clay, around 800g (1¾lb) for a small lampshade or more if you want to go larger
Wooden bat
Callipers
Ruler
Loop tools
Needle tool
Knife tool
Cutting wire
Sponge and water

olive bay laurel

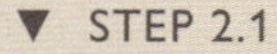

▼ STEP 1

▼ STEP 2.1

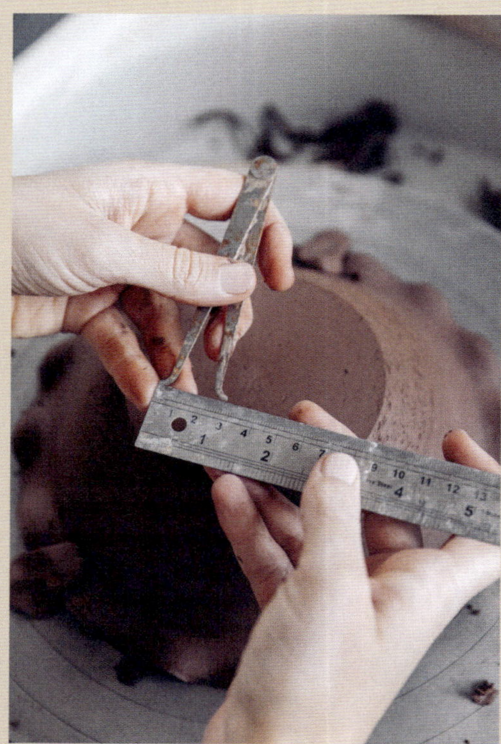

▲ STEP 5

▲ STEP 7

▼ STEP 2.2

▼ STEP 2.3

▲ STEP 9

▲ STEP 10

THROWING

1. Throw a large, wide bowl following the instructions on page 98, ensuring there is enough space to trim into the base later for the light fitting. Also make sure that there is sufficient space for your chosen light bulb, especially if you have a large or wide bulb in mind.

2. Shape the bowl to fit with your drawing or vision. Pictured are two examples for how to approach the design of your lampshade – adding a wavy edge or alternatively a flat flange. I created the wavy edge to my bowl by first creating a flat flange, and then shaping the rim as for the bowl on page 57.

3. Finish the lampshade by cleaning it up with a sponge, creating a chamfer under the base, and wiring through. Lift the bat off the wheel and allow the bowl to dry to leather hard.

TRIMMING

4. Centre the lampshade upside down and adhere it to the wheel head following the instructions on page 42.

5. If you have a small set of callipers, measure these to half the size of your light fitting, with shrinkage added to this measurement.

6. Find the very centre of your pot and, using your callipers like a compass, draw a circle. Press one arm of the callipers in the middle, holding them steady as the wheel spins. The other arm will draw a ring on the base of the bowl.

7. Double check this measurement with a ruler.

8. Trim the exterior form of the lampshade, just as you would a bowl. You can make the footring very large if you have enough clay, as long as it will fit the light fitting inside.

9. Hold the square corner of your loop tool, a needle or knife tool, steady in one spot while the wheel is spinning. This will slowly cut all the way through the base, leaving a hole.

10. Clean up the exterior wall with trimming tools and sponge off the piece.

GLAZING AND FITTING

11. When it comes to glazing your lampshade, be ready for a bit of a mission. Because it has no base, the usual trick of filling it up and tipping it out won't work. I glazed mine by blocking the hole with my palm, holding it for a few seconds, and then removing my hand quickly to let it all drain out. You may need someone to help you with this. You can also try painting the glaze on, although test out how the finish looks if you usually dip and pour.

12. Once fired, screw the light fitting and bulb onto your lampshade and switch it on!

Note:
I was using a coarse clay when I made this lampshade. I burnished some of the texture away using the back of a spoon as seen in image labelled step 10.

MOON JAR

A moon jar is a wonderful, striking style of pot. This is an iconic and traditional Korean jar made by joining one bowl to another. To me, this type of jar symbolizes a peaceful and solid union – the two halves of a whole.

Many potters make moon jars with the clay wetter and more malleable than I do. I prefer using my trimming tools to create the short neck, rather than throwing it. This possibly goes against the traditional way of making a moon jar, but it is the way I have always done it.

This jar can be thrown in one piece if you scale down but the aim of this project is to practice precision in throwing to a measured shape, joining clay and finessing a form.

It's important to throw the two halves one after the other, so that they shrink at the exact same rate.

I like making spherical moon jars, but they do not need to be perfectly round. Either way, it may help to draw some different shapes of jars and then decide on a shape that you like, even if it ends up being a sphere. You can draw a line through the middle of the drawing of your chosen jar to see the shape that each of the bowls need to be.

Materials and tools

Clay, two balls of clay of equal weight approx. 1000–1500g (2¼lb–3¼lb)
Bat
Ruler
Callipers
Teardrop and double-ended loop tools
Scoring tool
Serrated rib
Smooth metal or rubber rib
Needle or knife tool
Chuck and lugs
Cutting wire
Sponge and water

THROWING THE BOWLS

1. Centre one of your clay balls on a bat.
2. Throw a large, deep bowl following the instructions on page 102.
3. Once you have thrown the bowl, shape it so the external form matches what you have drawn, or to a shape that you are happy with. Ensure that the rim is reasonably chunky – approximately 0.8–1cm (⅜in) or so. If it's too thin, it will distort or crack when drying.
4. Measure the bowl with a ruler and note down the exact diameter of the rim. Mark the shape with callipers if you have them.
5. Clean up with a sponge, create a chamfer under the base, and wire through. Lift the bat off the wheel.
6. Repeat steps 1–5 for the second bowl, matching the size and shape of the first bowl as far as possible. Crucially, ensure the diameters of each rim are exactly the same.
7. Let the two bowls firm up to a very soft leather hard. If it is warm in your studio, keep an eye on the rims especially, and wrap them in plastic if they firm up but you are not ready to continue with the next steps.

JOINING THE BOWLS

When your bowls have firmed up – when they are holding their shape and are no longer sticky with wet clay – it's time to join the two pieces.

8. Remove both bowls from the bats using a wire. Select which of your bowls will be the base (bowl A), and the top (bowl B).
9. Centre and adhere bowl A, base down, to the wheel head, either with lugs or the slip method, following the instructions on pages 42–43.
10. Using a scoring tool, score the entire rim of both bowls, then paint a generous layer of slip on bowl A, all the way around the rim.
11. Tip bowl B over, and line its rim up with the rim of bowl A.
12. Once they are lined up, start pressing the clay from one side into the other. The air enclosed in the jar will help to support the form while you do this.
13. Using a serrated rib, begin to merge the two sides of the bowls together. Go all the way around the jar, scraping from one side of the join to the other.
14. Go over the marks left by the serrated rib with a smooth one. Use your preference of either metal or rubber, and smooth the marks left by joining. This process helps to merge the two bowls into one strong one.
15. You can add a tiny coil of clay to the join if you feel it is not sufficiently strong, and repeat step 13 to merge the clay together.

TRIMMING

16. With the two bowls now joined, and the base adhered to the wheel, begin trimming the neck into the moon jar. Much like trimming a footring, use the trimming tools to draw out where you would like the opening of the jar, and where you would like the neck to begin.
17. Trim away the sides of the neck.
18. With a needle or knife tool, cut a hole into the top of the moon jar. Hold the needle firmly in one spot as the wheel spins, very slowly pressing it down into the clay. This will cut a hole into the jar. Remove the disc of clay – ideally, just before it falls into the jar. If you miss it, you can shake it out later or use the needle to spear it out.
19. If you can reach your hand into the hole, tidy the internal join with a damp sponge. If you cannot, use a sponge on a stick to tidy it up.
20. Finesse the inner wall of the opening, the neck and the shoulder of the jar with trimming tools.
21. Measure or set a pair of callipers to the outer walls of the neck, as this will be replicated in the footring.

▼ STEP 2

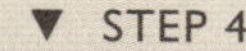

▼ STEP 4

▲ STEP 10.1

▲ STEP 10.2

▼ STEP 11

▼ STEP 13

▲ STEP 16

▲ STEP 18.1

▼ STEP 14

22. Remove the jar from the wheel.
23. Place a large chuck on the wheel and secure it with lugs. I don't have a large enough thrown chuck, so I used a plant pot with a soft tea towel draped inside to hold my moon jar.
24. Using the measurement of the neck, draw out where you would like to trim your footring (see page 46), and remove all excess clay. Generally, both the neck and footring are approximately the same measurements, but use this as a guide and not a rule, as your pot may suit something wider or narrower.
25. Finish the jar by sponging it down and removing it from the chuck.
26. Remove the chuck from the wheel, flip the jar over, and sponge the top off to remove any marks left from the chuck.
27. Let the jar dry very slowly, with a little plastic draped over to ensure the join does not crack.

▲ STEP 18.2

CAKE STAND

A handmade cake is best served on a handmade cake stand. It just makes a celebration that much more special!

Throwing a cake stand will not only help you learn how to handle larger quantities of clay, but also teach you a new skill – centring a second ball of clay onto the first. It feels very weird. It's also a bit of a mental challenge, as you throw the stand upside down. You have to consider how it will be flipped over at every stage. To help with this, you may want to have a second bat handy that you can hold over the cake stand to help visualize what it will look like when finished. My cake stand is 25cm (10in) in diameter and 15cm (6in) high.

Materials and tools

Clay, one 1300g (2¾lb) ball and one 400g (14oz) ball
Bat
Large, wide bat
Rib
Loop tools
Cutting wire
Sponge and water

THROWING

1. Attach a large, wide bat to the wheel head and then centre the larger ball of clay on the bat.
2. Throw a wide plate following the instructions on page 90. Keep the plate reasonably thick at this stage – at the very least 1cm (⅜in). If it is too thin, it will likely warp or crack. Leave enough clay at the edge to create a lip.
3. Use a rib to remove as much water and slip as possible.
4. Turn the wheel off and place the second ball of clay in the middle of the plate. Press it down firmly.
5. Turn the wheel on again and centre the smaller ball of clay on top of the thrown plate to become the stand.
6. Open the clay until you reach the same depth as the plate. Widen to approx. half the diameter of the plate measurement – although this is a guide and you can decide what you like the look of.
7. Pull up the walls from the base plate. Taper them outwards to ensure a well-balanced cake stand, using a rib to help if needed.
8. Ensure that the area where the stand joins onto the plate is not thicker than 2cm (¾in) in any area. This will lead to cracks in drying or firing.
9. Once the stand has been pulled up, move onto the lip of the plate. Pull up the extra clay on the lip. This is a design feature, not a functional one, so you can play with what this looks like. Adding something like a ripple to the lip is a possibility, or you could follow a similar shape to the stand.

▼ STEP 2

▼ STEP 4

▲ STEP 7.2

▲ STEP 12

▼ STEP 7.1

▲ STEP 17

10. Finish the cake stand by removing all excess water from the plate and inside the stand. Make a small chamfer under the base and pull your wire under to cut the cake stand off the bat. Note that something very wide can be difficult to cut off: slowly spin the wheel while wiring off to help. Make sure that your wire is held very tight.

TRIMMING

Keep an eye on the cake stand as it dries. If it is adhered to the bat, but is dry enough to trim, it can be helpful to leave it there during steps 11–13.

11. Centre and attach the cake stand, still upside down, to the wheel head (see page 42).
12. Trim any excess clay from the stand, the base of the plate, the lip and around the join. Ensure that no part of the cake stand is thicker than 2cm (¾in).
13. Tidy everything up with a sponge.
14. Flip the cake stand over, and centre it again, right way up, then adhere it to the wheel head.
15. Trim off any excess clay from the top of the plate. There may not be much excess at all, but use this opportunity to tidy and finish the plate and lip with your trimming tools.
16. Create the tiniest of chamfers on the edge of the lip, which will help to avoid any chipping once the cake stand is glazed and fired.
17. Use a sponge to remove trimming marks.
18. Remove the cake stand from the wheel, drape it with some plastic and allow it to dry slowly.

Tip

- If you find that your cake stand warps or cracks at the join, you may need to have a wider base or thicker plate. This is a complex ask of the clay, so be prepared to try it a few times if it doesn't work straight away.

TWO-PART VASE

The last, but certainly not least, project is a two-part vase. I first created a vase like this after a trip to Italy. I visited a museum which was exhibiting ancient bone china, and the forms and intricacies of the decoration really took my interest. I stood, staring at little details like the join of a handle or the ripple of a lip, for what felt like hours.

After this trip, I went home and made a few of these pieces in my own clay and style. This began a years-long series, lovingly dubbed the Florence Series, named after the trip, but also a nod to my niece, also named Florence.

I make these vases in two (sometimes three!) parts. I throw a few different components all at once, and then, once leather hard, I puzzle them together to decide which ones look best together. It's important to throw these pieces in the same session so that they shrink at exactly the same rate.

It helps to draw a few vases to begin with, and to section them off into two parts: base and neck. Doing this will help when it comes to shaping the clay, as you will already have a visual reference when throwing.

Throw this project on a bat.

Materials and tools

Clay, one 1000g (2¼lb) ball and one 500g (1lb) ball
Bat
Rib
Ruler or callipers
Lugs
Loop tools
Needle tool
Cutting wire
Sponge and water

THROWING

Base

1. Attach a bat to the wheel head and centre the larger piece of clay on top.
2. Section off around 1.5cm (⅝in) at the base of the centred ball of clay. Throw a tall cylinder following the instructions on page 28, leaving the base of clay at the wheel head.
3. When you are pulling up the walls, consider the shape of your piece, and allow the clay to move into this shape while you are pulling. It is easy to let the shoulder become too thin, so ensure that you have an even thickness of clay from base to rim.
4. Once the desired height is achieved, shape the base of the vase with your sponge, a rib and your fingers.
5. Measure the opening of the vase with a ruler or callipers.
6. Finish the piece by cleaning up with a sponge, creating a chamfer under the base, and wiring through. Lift the bat off the wheel.

Neck

7. Attach a bat to the wheel head and centre the smaller piece of clay on top to create the neck of the vase.

8. Open this piece all the way to the bat and widen. It must be slightly wider than the opening of the neck of the vase.

9. Pull up the wall and shape it so it has a slight curve inwards and then back out.

10. Double check the measurement on the outside.

11. Finish the neck by cleaning up with a sponge, creating a chamfer under the base and wiring through. Lift the bat off the wheel.

12. Hold the neck section above the base of the vase to check you are happy with the overall form. If you think the two pieces don't quite match up, try to decide why that is, and repeat steps 7–11 to throw another neck which better suits the base. You may need more or less clay to achieve this goal.

13. Let both the neck and the base dry to a soft leather hard.

TRIMMING AND JOINING

14. Make a few long handles following the steps on pages 50–52. Shape them and set them aside to firm up while trimming. I made a slab handle, but a pulled handle would look very elegant and at home on this style of vase. I find it useful to have a few different handles in case I like the form of one better or I make a mistake and want to start over. Leave these to dry a little whilst you are trimming and attaching the vase.

15. Centre and attach the neck, upside down, to the wheel head. Secure with lugs of clay.

16. Place the base of the vase on top of the neck and look at the way that they should join.

17. Try to match the angle of the shoulder of the base to the neck by trimming the negative of this angle. Periodically test this by placing the base on the neck to see if it sits flush.

18. Once flush, place the base on the neck and ensure it is centred and sitting correctly. Once it is all lined up, take a needle tool and create registration marks on the two parts of the vase in a few different places. I like to mark with a line, a circle and a cross.

19. Remove the base, and score both the neck and the base thoroughly. Generously apply slip to the neck.

20. Place the base back on the neck and align both sides using the registration marks. Press the neck into the shoulder of the vase to join the two parts.

21. Blend the join using a rib. If you are having trouble blending the join completely, follow the steps for attaching the two parts of the Moon Jar on page 146. If you find that there is a gap or a step of clay, you may also like to add a small coil of clay to the join to help blend it out.

22. Stand up and trim a footring into the base of the vase (see page 46).

23. Trim any other areas of excess clay and soften with a damp sponge.

24. Carefully turn the piece over and attach the handle to the vase following the instructions on page 53.

25. Allow the vase to dry slowly, with some plastic draped over the top.

Tips

- Once you have attached the neck to the base, be very careful not to knock the vase over or let the clay catch while you trim: the join is very fragile, and the piece now has a high centre of gravity, making it liable to toppling over.
- If you find that your handle is sagging, you can prop it up with some clay, or something else that is soft enough to move while it is drying – balled-up tissue paper works well.

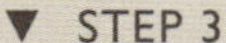

▼ STEP 1

▼ STEP 3

▲ STEP 4

▲ STEP 5

▼ STEP 10

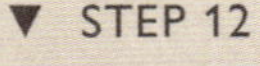

▼ STEP 12

▲ STEP 18.2

▲ STEP 19

▼ STEP 17

▼ STEP 18.1

▲ STEP 22

▲ STEP 24

ABOUT THE AUTHOR

Lilly Maetzig is the potter behind London based ceramics brand, Mae Ceramics. She loves making beautiful, enjoyable, useful pieces that people use in their everyday lives. A big part of her practice is teaching – online, in person, and in writing.

Lilly Maetzig is also the author of *Handbuilt: A Modern Potter's Guide To Handbuilding With Clay.*

ACKNOWLEDGEMENTS

I am very thankful to a lot of people for the creation of this book.

Firstly, to the pottery community and my supporters and followers. Thank you so much for buying my pots, books and courses, for watching my videos and liking my posts online. That support has got me to where I am, and I am very lucky to have such a kind group of people behind me.

To my family and friends who've and always believed that I'd have success in something creative – sometimes more belief than I've had in myself!

To the Edwardses who watch every video, and read every word I write – thank you. To Karlee who has always talked me through any doubts, and to my lovely Dad who reckons I'd be no potter without him. Not sure about that Pops, but I'm grateful for your support nonetheless.

Very grateful to my publishing team – Gemma, India, Charlie and especially Harriet. Sorry for never replying to emails on time, thanks for still publishing me!

And last – but absolutely not least – always thankful to my Jack for your endless support and kindness. Love you.

Studio photos taken with permission at Second Floor Studios, London.